CROSSING BACK OVER
THE PRACTICE OF
OWNING AND ACCEPTING
BIPOLAR DISORDER

BRETT STEVENS

PAGE PUBLISHING, INC.
Conneaut Lake, PA

First originally published by Page Publishing 2020

Some of the names and identifying details have been
changed to protect the privacy of individuals.

ISBN 978-1-6624-1451-0 (pbk)
ISBN 978-1-6624-1453-4 (hc)
ISBN 978-1-6624-1452-7 (digital)

Printed in the United States of America

Patience: the capacity to accept or tolerate delay, trouble, or suffering without getting angry or upset.

Waiting: the action of staying where one is or delaying action until a particular time or until something else happens.

"How I remember it..."

YOU

"You have bipolar disorder."

I heard the doctor say the words but felt nothing. I was frozen but used my parents' reactions as a gauge for how upset I should be. My mom was shredding through her notepad, writing furiously, while concern was written on her face. My dad was calm and asking questions nonchalantly like we were here for a normal checkup. *Say ah!* Truthfully, I was more embarrassed that my parents were doing the talking for me than receiving the diagnosis and news that I'd have to take medication for the rest of my life. The three manic episodes and family history of mental illness that were just described to the doctor must have qualified me for the diagnosis. *You have bipolar disorder.*

"One hundred percent of people with bipolar disorder who do not stay on their medication will relapse," the doctor said.

You have bipolar disorder. Then he took out a small, rectangular slip of medical-looking paper and scribbled on it. He said a lot of words, but all I heard was "lithium." My dad was confident and took the slip, which made me more skeptical because he knew something that my mom and I didn't. So what if my dad was also a doctor? *You have bipolar disorder.* I needed to get out of the small office and learn more about how my life was falling apart, at least there would be fresh air.

The only task in my entire world at that moment was to follow my dad. This was very difficult for me after living independently out of state and not having consistent contact with him for years. *I have bipolar disorder.* The chronic brain disorder that caused one to not live in reality was becoming more real to me. We took a short drive to get blood work done, where I learned something about needing to get this done regularly to make sure the lithium wouldn't shut down my kidneys and kill me. I played it super cool externally until I was sitting with my sleeve pulled up awaiting a needle to pull blood. *Is this part of bipolar disorder?* I was scared that this was my new life. I started having a similar experience that I had a few weeks ago where I had a panic attack in the psychiatric hospital. I thought I was going to die. Thinking about this thought made it worse and the cycle continued. I became light-headed and nervous as the blood flowed out of my arm. I tried to breath and scrunched my foot for what I thought would pump more blood to the rest of my body, an attempt at getting creative. Finally, it was over, and I had fulfilled my one and only responsibility. I didn't understand or have insight into what the next one would be. So I followed again. Followed my parents like a twenty-nine-year-old child on a leash until I ended up back at my mom's place.

My dad left, and I was alone with my mom. I wasn't depressed yet, but it was depressing to be there. This wasn't my home. My gaze now focused more on my mom, and I noticed the fear in her. She reviewed her notes and made sure I had the appropriate medication. I thought about how I had felt this exact way twice before but without the bipolar label. They called those two episodes Psychotic Disorder NOS. I recalled the discussion with the doctor that the chronic brain disorder was associated with multiple manic episodes and family history, but how would that information help me now? How would that help me get through today? Tonight? Forever?

I scanned the room and honed in on the fridge. I ate everything in it and forgot that I had bipolar disorder for a minute. Then I raided the pantry and found a similar feeling of relief. My mom sat with me until it was med time. *This is definitely part of bipolar disorder.* I had to take nine pills that night, and I chose to go one at a time because I wouldn't choke that way, which extended the uncomfortable task and made me feel foolish. I had zoned out when the doctor explained to me how the collage of pills work, so I had to place my trust in my mom. It didn't have to be blind trust, but it was because

6

I didn't want to think or learn anything new. *If I'm so disabled right now, then you can tell me what to do!*

I lay in bed that night, drugged up, and drowsy, thinking about the past and wondering about the future. My tough guy persona disappeared, and it was finally time for me to be afraid. I felt an ache in my stomach and thought my kidney had shut down. I was thirsty and had to pee at the same time. The voices in my head were organizing themselves and continued to spit out one question. *What is bipolar disorder?* I was about to find out.

THE BUZZ

When I woke up the next morning, I knew that hell isn't a place you go; it's a feeling that lives inside you. For me, it was a panicky buzz that was lodged all the way down my throat and into my belly. *Is this what my life is like now?* I was fixated on and very aware that bipolar disorder is forever. My eyes scanned the room without my head moving, and I was reminded that I was home again. Home, in the same town where I grew up. Home, without a job and dependent on my mom again. Home, afraid of the rest of the world. I screamed at the top of my lungs silently inside my head.

I desperately tried to remind myself that having a full day with nothing to do was sort of like a day off. I thought about all the things that I'd always enjoyed while off from work or school. *Well, I could start my day with a nice breakfast, then head to the gym, then call a friend, watch a movie, play chess, mess with some online poker maybe, have a nice dinner.* But the hell-like buzz kept me glued to the bed. The more I tried to get up, the harder my thoughts pinned me like a professional wrestler in the ring. *One, two, three, it's over!*

Then I forgot about regular activities and made a mental list of tasks that were required for survival. *Food, water, and medicine.* Although dying didn't seem so bad, I did not want to die. *How do I not die? Food, water, and medicine.* But none of those were within arm's reach of my bed, so the panic and fear got worse. *How will I ever take care of myself with this hell inside of me?* Then I heard my mom's footsteps downstairs and experienced a warm feeling that doused water on the flame of the internal fiery hell of anxiety that I felt. My mom loved me unconditionally. I noticed the warm-looking carpet on the floor and found the courage to put my bare foot on it, my first real step with bipolar disorder.

After a few steps to the bathroom, I took a look at myself in the mirror. *What a mess you are.* My hair had that ugly bed head look to it, there were needle marks in my arm from the mess of blood work and tests done in the last week, and I didn't recognize the look in my own eyes. It was important that I beat myself up a little more and take the blame for all this. *What are you gonna do about this, Brett?*

I used the bathroom and chugged water out of the faucet like I had been in the desert for weeks. The panic faded, and my dark thoughts fell back temporarily, maybe because I got out of bed or maybe because of the hydration. *This water is surprisingly good. What else will be better now?* I tried to think of other things that might be better than before being tagged as an individual with bipolar disorder but came up empty. Then I felt a bit nauseated after the moment of relief. *Do I have the flu? What is in that medicine? Is this bipolar disorder?*

I could smell breakfast, which motivated me to move toward the staircase. I took a hard step with my right foot, and the short hallway rotated to the right. I took a step with my left foot, and the short hallway rotated to the left. I had a flashback to turning the whole world with my steps in Texas ten days ago and in the hospital last week. *I'm certainly still in hell.* Like in the hospital, I used the wall for support and followed the smell of breakfast.

"Good morning. How are you, Brett?" my mom asked, still frying eggs.

"I'm fine," I answered quickly. It required way less effort to answer this way than to run through what it was like to get out of bed a few minutes ago.

"I laid your meds out for you, and breakfast is almost done. Go have a seat at the table. You have to eat breakfast before taking your meds." I walked slowly over to the table and sat down.

Breakfast was easy to eat, but the first taste made me want coffee. *They told me not to drink alcohol or do drugs. There is no way caffeine is good for me.* I thought about how many cups of coffee I'd have back in Texas before leading my team at work as the director of operations at a fast-growing, successful start-up. *I guess being motivated and energetic is bad for me now.*

"I made you decaf coffee if you want some," my mom voiced from the kitchen.

She was a step ahead on that one. I had a sip and noticed how bad it was compared to real coffee. *This is my life now, lukewarm and tasteless.* Then came the meds again. Like last night, I didn't ask any questions. I took each of the nine pills individually like a failing trainee on day one at work. It was pathetic. But I had completed the survival tasks this morning. *Food, water, and medicine.* It was 9:00 a.m. *Now what?*

RESTLESSNESS

"Do you need anything at the moment? I'm going to take a shower," my mom asked.

"No," I replied with an attitude. *Why is she trying so hard? I'm an adult.* I felt alone while she was in the kitchen with me, but now I was physically alone in this quiet house as she went upstairs. *It's 9:01 a.m. Did all that just happen in a minute?* I remained seated and stared at the clock to get a sense of what a new minute felt like.

An uncomfortable itch bounced around my body, making it hard to sit still. This urged me to get out of the chair and put my plate in the sink. I took another few gulps of water out of the faucet, which wasn't nearly as pleasurable as my first taste upstairs after waking up. *Even water is dull again, ugh.* The itchy feeling went away momentarily but came back after my mind had a second to start thinking. *It's 9:05 a.m., wow! Slow start here.* I had a sense that there would be food, water, and medicine sometime around noon. *Long way to go.* I saw a book out of the corner of my eye, *Siddhartha* by Hermann Hesse. My dad had urged me to read this book years ago, and it was short, so I sat down. Siddhartha *by Herman.* The itch bounced around my body and took my focus, not that I was very focused to begin with. *Not doing this.* I closed the book. *It's 9:10 a.m.* I tossed the book aside and went for the remote.

I'd been the leading character of every television station ten days ago in Texas. News anchors, weather reporters, actors, and reality stars—they were all talking about me through the TV, and I wondered if they still cared about me after my hospitalization. Another punch of panic hit me as I pressed the power button on the remote control.

A news anchor was reporting, *Wow, just wow. This kid actually thought we were talking about him the whole time? He must be dumb. Have fun at home, Brett!*

Fuck off. I was ready to fight the man on the TV, but then a beam of sunshine shed through the window, a reminder from God to settle down. I turned off the TV. *It's 9:15 a.m.*

I was breathing heavily now, feeling like I had exhausted all my options in fifteen minutes and dealing with a restless itch moving from my toes to my head to my arms and back again. *Working out might help.* I got down in a push-up position and did a few. *Ouch, that sucked.* I went to the pantry and downed a whole bag of marshmallows, sarcastically laughing to myself and feeling my physical body slipping away from me as well. *I earned these marshmallows after two push-ups, right?* I laughed again. I retraced my activities over the last twenty minutes. *I already cleaned up after myself, tried to read a book, tried to watch TV, tried to work out, and snacked. Definitely snacked. Didn't have to try at all to do that.* I heard the shower stop running upstairs. *She must be done in there.* I thought that showering might be a reasonable thing to do next.

I had to pass the mirror again to make it into the shower, where I found more evidence that I was pathetic. As the warm water crashed into my back, I had more time to think and more time to remember where I showered last week—in the psychiatric hospital—and what it was like. I saw flashes of straitjackets, treadmills, birds, and pizza— all symbols during my manic episodes. I didn't trust my own mind and had no plan moving forward. When I got out of the shower and came downstairs, my mom challenged me to a game of gin rummy. *What's the point?*

"Fine, I'll go easy on you," I said with a partial smile that was close to what my smiles used to be like. She won, and I challenged her to a game of chess even without her fully knowing the rules. *Maybe I can teach my mom how to become a grandmaster.* The thought of having some sort of purpose gave me a good feeling, the best one that I had had all day. Then the warmth was disrupted by real questions. *How am I ever going to work again? I can't just teach my mom how to play chess for the rest of my life. How am I going to make money? I won't make any money teaching my mom chess for the rest of my life.* No matter what positive thought came, it was crushed by a pouring out of unknowns. I lost track of time during our game and looked at the clock. *It's 11:45 a.m.* Time for lunch.

HOLDING ON

The rest of the day and the next couple weeks were about the same. I'd struggle to find things to do and complain about my life being a train wreck compared to what it once was. As time passed, there was more discussion about what happened back in Texas. When I was deep inside my manic episode, I thought I knew everything. I didn't have to answer to anyone. I was special and could speak directly with God. Now I was being asked questions like "Are you sure you didn't smoke any weed?" and "I found a lot of empty bottles of liquor in your kitchen. Are you sure you weren't drinking too much?" I became frustrated with my mom. *Just because I lost my mind, it doesn't mean I'm lying to you!* I had no sense of where she was coming from because I wasn't able to see that my previous two episodes had been induced by marijuana. I also didn't appreciate how she was reporting my status back to other family members.

"He seems okay today. Just a little off."

My blood would boil in the other room. *Yeah, everything is perfect!*

One evening I was attempting to fall asleep and the restlessness kicked in again, overpowering the medication that helped me sleep. My mind was stuck on the trauma from the hospital, and I thought my mom should know what it was like on the inside. I asked her to sit downstairs with me and listen.

"Mom, I'm actually proud of myself for what I had to do to get out of there. Have you ever been confined like that? Have you ever had an experience like I did? After the first day, I had the whole place working for me. I knew where everyone was going to be at all times. I had to pretend to follow the orders of the staff, but I was really doing what I had to do to survive. When you would leave after visiting hours is when it got scary and dangerous. But I made it. I know what it's like. How could you possibly have thought that they were nice people in there? Why were you having me sign papers to give you and dad authority to make decisions for me? That made it way harder and more confusing. Why did you bring cookies to the front desk? That may have seemed like the right thing to do in your sheltered world, but do you know what happened the second you left? Huh? My floor-mates started to tease and call me a little bitch. That was your fault. And you know what else? They saw how you guys dress and how you flaunt your wealth. They know people outside of the hospital who would have robbed you if I didn't step in after you left. It wasn't easy! You brought me sushi? I had to kick people out of a community room so we could eat. I paid a price for that later by getting looks in the dining area. Oh, and when I'm finally ready to leave, discharged after all this bullshit, I give clothes that I don't need to people who are homeless on the unit and have nowhere to go, and you tell me to go back up to the floor and take them back? What is wrong with you?"

I was pumping myself up and getting buzzed off this release of anger and continued, "I knew that place inside out and could predict what everyone was going to do, when they were going to do it. Extraordinary things really were happening that can't be explained! People really were talking behind my back! One day the whole world will be talking about me. This is how I'm being groomed!" I was breathing heavily.

"I hear what you are saying, Brett. And I'm sorry if I made it harder for you." She was a bit emotional, but that didn't change my mood. Then I saw her sorting through paperwork, looking for a phone number. "I think we need a little more help," she said to me.

"Fine," I said, willing to comply but still feeling like everything I had just said was fair game.

She found the number of a psychologist that was referred by my psychiatrist that would focus more on my emotional state and less on medication. I gave him a call the next morning as a favor to my mom.

MISBEHAVING

"Put it on speaker," she said. I gave her a look and placed the phone on the dining room table so we could both hear the call.

"What's his name again?" I asked.

"Uh." She hustled over to the kitchen to find her notes.

A man with a warm voice answered, "This is Dr. E."

I gave my mom a look. *Thanks for being so prepared!* "Uh, hi, Dr. E. My name is Brett, and I got your number from Dr. D."

"Tell him you saw Dr. D yesterday and that your last name is Stevens," my mom whispered.

Dr. E started talking again, and I leaned back in my chair, frustrated with my mom. *I can't do two things at once!*

"Hi, Brett," he replied.

"I was hoping to schedule an appointment with you when you get a chance," I said.

"Tell him it has to be as soon as possible!" my mom mouthed silently.

Ugh, please stop distracting me.

"We can do that," he replied. "How about next week?"

"Next week would be fine." I felt a slight sense of pride that I could make this appointment independently while also navigating my mom's distractions.

"Next week isn't soon enough!" she said a little louder.

This pushed me over the edge. I looked at her with pure disgust. "Fine, you make the appointment then!" I handed her the phone and bolted out of my seat. I heard her apologize to Dr. E. Then I met her back at the table and said, "Do you realize I can't talk to both of you at the same time?"

"Next week is too far away," she replied, frustrated with me.

The whole situation reminded me that I was dependent on her, but I should've been able to make a phone call without her breathing down my neck. I overcompensated later that night by asking if I could drive to the casino and play poker by myself. *I have to ask now? Ugh.* In my early twenties, I was a professional poker player. The game was more therapeutic at this point in my life and less about making money.

"No," she said. "Let's do something else."

Are you serious? "Why?" I asked.

"Brett, I think we both know why. It's been a long day. Can we please just find something else to do?"

"No," I replied. "I'm twenty-nine years old and should be able to go to the casino if I want to go to the casino. I'm taking your car."

She became angry. "Fine, Brett, you want to go to the casino? I'll come with you."

"Fine, I said."

The thirty-minute drive was somewhat quiet when we went to the casino. I was fine until we entered the main floor where there were loud noises and flashing lights. I felt dizzy and lost the confidence that I had shown before the trip. *Don't let her see that you are scared. That would be pathetic.* She stood beside me as I withdrew $300 from the ATM.

"That fee is ridiculous!" she said.

Then we went to the poker room, and I looked around at the full tables. I was overstimulated and somewhat buzzed as I traded in three one-hundred-dollar bills for three stacks of red five-dollar chips. I took a seat at a table, with her in a chair behind me as one of the only females in the room.

Then I was back at the World Series of Poker Main Event featured table in Las Vegas that I had played a few years ago. My mind had kicked back into manic mode and took a break from being lethargic and depressed. *Blinds are $1/$3, and I have $300 chips and one hundred big blinds. I'm on the button with one player raising from under* *the gun to ten dollars. I'm holding Ks-Js, a call behind hand according to my code.* "Call," I said as I threw in ten dollars. *Both players folded on my left, and the flop is Qh-10c-2s. The pot now has one dollar, plus three dollars for the blinds, plus ten dollars for the first raise, plus ten dollars for my call, which is equal to twenty-four dollars. The other player in the hand has about $600 worth of chips. He bets fifteen dollars. I have a mediocre hand, and according to my code, I should call with fifteen dollars. There is now twenty-four dollars, plus fifteen dollars, plus fifteen dollars in the pot, which is equal to fifty-four dollars. The next card is the Ac. Bingo. He bets forty dollars, and I raise to one hundred dollars. He moves all in.* "Call," I said, looking back at my mom with a smirk as I pulled in the pot of $604. She shook her head and laughed.

We left the casino around 10:30 p.m., which was too late, especially because my medicine was at home and I was supposed to take it at 9:00 p.m. The excess stimulation had caught up with me, and my mind would not stop churning on the drive home. When I lay down in bed that night, my brain would not turn off. I could not fall asleep. But there was less panic tonight. I felt a hint of confidence that my poker game was still on point. I stared at the ceiling with my eyes wide open and heart pounding for most of the night. My $604 cash sat next to my bed.

THE PUZZLE

I came down from whatever poker high I was on the next morning, and the familiar hell-like buzz was back. *This must be bipolar. Why is this happening?* I looked at the cash next to me in disgust and blamed myself for staying out late. When I choked down my morning pills, I was reminded that I didn't take the meds at the correct time last night. *Nice one, Brett!* I felt a bit nauseated and hated the idea of spending the entire day alone with my mom again. *What can I do? What can I do?* Nothing came to me. *This is terrible.* "Mom! What should I do today? This is terrible!"

"How about gin rummy?"

"No."

"Want to teach me more chess?"

"No."

"Why don't you help me make lunch?"

"Absolutely not."

"I think there may be puzzles downstairs." *Fine.*

We had a few smaller puzzles in the basement, and I completed them as my "full-time job" over the next day or so. There was nothing else to do. I liked doing puzzles because I didn't have to talk to anyone or leave the house. *These aren't hard enough. I need a harder puzzle.* I had a thought that reminded me of my old self. I had no interest in researching puzzles in any way, but I knew there was a Barnes & Noble a few miles up the road at the mall. *Don't be a pussy Brett. Be a man, walk to the car, go to Barnes & Noble, buy a puzzle, come back home to your pathetic life.* I saw the keys on the counter and could have listened to my thoughts. But for some reason "Mom, can I take the car to Barnes & Noble to get a new puzzle?" came out. *There's dependent Brett again.* She came tumbling down the stairs.

"Are you sure you feel okay to drive all by yourself? Do you want me to come with you?" she asked.

I'm a child. I didn't like the questions, but at least I saw where she was coming from this time. I had, after all, explained to her how I had driven 110 miles on the highway, drove out of the Enter in a packed parking lot, and flew through green and red lights in the middle of the downtown city late at night in Texas about a month ago.

"Mom, if I'm ever going to be independent ever again, then I'm going to have to be able to do things like this on my own." She gave me a hug along with the keys to her car.

My confidence faded when I turned the engine on and the radio was evaluating my conversation upstairs with my mom. *Is it such a big deal to drive yourself somewhere? Why are you letting her control you like that?* It all felt real, but I didn't analyze it because I was so used to these types of hallucinations at this point. I didn't connect that it might have something to do with my medication not being correct. I timidly drove to the mall with both hands on the wheel and parked in the first open space that I saw.

As I started walking toward Barnes & Noble, I realized that there were many more open spots that were closer. I froze in the middle of the lot, confused. *Should I go back and move the car up? It's probably fine. But is it okay? Maybe I should move it up. Well, I don't know. Hmm.* I looked over and saw a group of teenagers looking at me. *Ugh, they are making fun of me. Make up your mind!* I ran back to the car and turned the engine on.

Make up your mind, Brett! You are embarrassing yourself, said the woman on the radio.

I pulled up a few more spaces and parked. I walked straight into Barnes & Noble to the game section, probably mumbling to myself. *Everyone shut up. Leave me alone.* There were even more people in the store staring at me. I felt panicky and went straight back to the games section. Thankfully, a five-thousand-piece puzzle of the Sistine Chapel was the first thing I saw. *Well, that's a big-ass puzzle. Let's do it.* I took it straight to the counter.

"Ninety dollars."

I took my card out, paid for the puzzle, and darted back to the car. I kept the radio off, but now the clouds were forming into faces in the sky, and streetlights were making meaningful patterns. Again, nothing I hadn't seen back in Texas.

I made it back home with my puzzle, frazzled. *Why was that so hard? Is this bipolar disorder?* I brought the large puzzle upstairs and was greeted by my mom.

"Brehhht, did you really have to get such a big puzzle? How much was that?" she asked.

"Ninety dollars," I replied.

"Brett, that's crazy!" she said.

"I can afford it!" I replied. I stopped listening and put the puzzle on the table with a slight interest in getting to work on it. *I'm going to finish this damn puzzle.*

Still Manic

It took an entire day to flip the pieces over, but eventually, I finished the border and was retraining my brain by working on the puzzle. I knew that finishing it would impress others, something that I had strived for my entire life. The problem with getting an old sense of myself back, however, was that my mood meter could easily tip in the other direction. *I'm amazing at this puzzle! I'm so good at organizing things! I feel like my old self! I'm not depressed anymore! I'm not bipolar anymore!* My mind would race and drown out the depression with feelings of elation.

My eyes shot open one morning with the pull of anxiety in my gut. *Puzzle.* I shot out of bed like a magician made me disappear, leaving the blanket falling onto the bed behind me. *Puzzle.* I hustled to the bathroom and doused my toothbrush with water under the sink. *Hurry up, hurry up, hurry up.* I brushed once or twice without toothpaste and practically sprinted down the stairs. *Puzzle, puzzle, puzzle.* I gobbled down a power bar and shot down my pills, still one at a time, which delayed puzzle time and bothered me. I saw my mom's lips moving, and I nodded but had no care or clue what words were coming out. Finally, I made it to the six-by-three dining room table where my future masterpiece lived. *Finally!*

A bird chirped, and I looked out of the window. I noticed the four corners of the window. My head shifted back to the puzzle, and I honed in on the four corners of the puzzle. *Take a deep breath. It's happening.* The letters F-O-U-R flashed in my head. *Four. Four what? F like f off?* I continued to scan the puzzle. I took a deep breath and had a slight awareness that my mind was doing something that was not useful to me; it was more entertaining. I was lucky to have another thought that I should tell someone about this experience that I'm having. *Who? Dr. E!* I snapped out of this mental circus and took a break from the puzzle.

"Mom!" I yelled, knowing she was upstairs.

"Yes, Brett?"

"Can we try going out to eat? I need some fresh air."

"Yes, Brett, anything you want. I'm proud of you." *Here we go again, getting a gold star for getting out of the house.*

I felt vulnerable going to lunch with my mom, much different from the forceful confidence I had when heading toward the casino. When we got to the restaurant, the first thing I heard was the hostess making fun of me for being a baby and needing my mommy to take me to lunch like a child.

"Ha ha." she giggled and made eye contact with me, delivering the message. *I am a loser.* Then I heard all the people at the tables making fun of me in the same manner.

Go home! Wow, what a good mom he has. What a loser.

I started to feel anxious but had a temporary reminder of the puzzle and how I was able to observe myself going down a rabbit hole earlier in the day. We started walking toward our table in the back. *Go home! Wow, what a good mom he has. What a loser.*

It's not real.

Go home! Wow, what a good mom he has. What a loser.

It's not real.

Go home! Wow, what a good mom he has. What a loser.

Nobody cares enough to make these remarks about me. It's not real. I took a deep breath and sat down. I was scared but learning something about my mind.

"You okay, Brett?" my mom asked. She must have been able to tell that I was experiencing some sort of discomfort.

"Yes, I'm fine." I felt stronger with her there.

We ordered some food, and I was able to create a mental bubble around the two of us. I pretended we were eating at home and anything outside the bubble was meaningless. I felt comfortable at that table, in my seat, at that restaurant, for that moment. When it was time to get up and leave, the bubble broke, and I experienced a few more cycles of *Go home! Wow, what a good mom he has. What a loser.*

It's not real.

Go home! Wow, what a good mom he has. What a loser.

It's not real.

Go home! Wow, what a good mom he has. What a loser.

Nobody cares enough to make these remarks about me, it's not real.

When we got back to the car, I was upset.

"What happened in there, Brett?" she asked.

"The whole room was talking about me! I know it isn't real, but it feels real. It's very uncomfortable, and it's not going away!"

She looked concerned, and we didn't discuss it very long, but we both knew that this information needed to be brought to the medical professionals.

DR. E

I'm sitting in a waiting room with mom on my right and Dad on my left, staring at the fuzzy gray carpet waiting to be called into Dr. E's office. The fuzzy gray carpet began to move and create a static image like when an old TV set wasn't plugged into the cable box yet. My ears started to buzz. *This is so cool. Is this bipolar disorder?*

"Brett? I will see you now," said Dr. E, breaking my concentration.

I stood up and made eye contact with him, feeling comforted by his gaze. My parents stayed behind, and the door closed behind us. A bird flew past the window. *Noted.* The clock changed. *Noted.*

"Please have a seat anywhere that you like," he said.

There were three options. A chair facing the window, a chair facing that chair, and a maroon couch facing both chairs. I stood for an extra second or two before making my choice. *The seat facing the window is his chair, the one he sees patients with. Why would he want me to sit there? The seat facing his chair is at eye level; wouldn't it be awkward to sit there? The couch looks like the obvious choice for where patients should sit, so why would he give me the option to sit anywhere else?* I had analyzed the seating situation but still had to decide what role I wanted to play here—the teacher, the student, or something in between. I took a seat on the maroon couch. *I'm the patient, and he's the professional. Done.* He sat down in his chair and got right to it, not terribly concerned with who sat where, but I was certain that I had passed his test. *Well done, B.*

Dr. E had a yellow notepad and number 2 pencil in hand, ready to roll. "So, Brett, what brings you here today?"

Didn't someone already tell this guy about my bipolar-ness? Technically, my parents brought me here. "Well, I was just diagnosed with bipolar disorder. Dr. D and my mom thought it would be a good idea to get some additional help for a little while."

"I see," he said. "How did you come into the diagnosis?" he asked.

I didn't come into anything. The diagnosis came into me! "I was living in Texas by myself in the downtown area of a major city. I was in charge of thirty-five employees in a start-up company that I worked for. Then out of nowhere, I had what I think they call a manic episode and was hospitalized and brought back home where I got the diagnosis from Dr. D."

He was taking notes like a madman, but I never got the sense that he wasn't listening to the new information I was spouting out as well.

"What happened during your manic episode?" he asked.

A bird flew past the window again. "Did you see that bird?" I asked.

"Yes," he replied. "I can see it out of the corner of my eye while I'm still talking to you. "So?" he said.

He doesn't get it. "Isn't it strange that for some reason my brain is making the bird important?"

He took more notes and asked, "Maybe it is and maybe it isn't, but is it useful information?"

Good point. "No, but it's fun to think this way."

"I can certainly see why that would be stimulating, but so are a lot of things, like drugs."

Thinking creatively is now a drug, bummer. "Yeah, that makes sense," I said, being a bit of a brownnose. I spent the next twenty minutes or so telling stories about my previous episodes having to do with birds, pickles, pizza, and streetlights as Dr. E took notes furiously.

"Okay, Brett, our time is almost up. Would you mind asking your parents to come in here?"

"Sure," I said. My parents came in, and we all shared the maroon couch now.

"Thanks for coming in. I agree with Dr. D that Brett has bipolar disorder."

Yeah, we all already knew that.

"I think working with him once or twice a week would be very beneficial."

What exactly are we working on?

"I also think it would be wise to have a neurological exam done to rule out any other reasons for these symptoms."

Oh boy.

I didn't break down to tears when receiving the news that I might have a brain issue along with bipolar disorder, but I was sad, and a tear swelled up behind my right eye. Dr. E made eye contact with my dad again like they both knew something that my mom and I didn't. *These docs really know it all, huh.* The next few minutes were a fog of words and phrases being exchanged between the nonbipolar individuals in the room, that I didn't pay much attention to. Then all three of them looked over at me.

"Any other questions, Brett?"

"No, I'm fine."

My mom, dad, and I had lunch at a nearby diner afterward, and the waitstaff and customers were all hoping for the best for me. *You can do it, Brett!* There were also a few who were hoping I would have brain cancer and die. *You can't do it, Brett!*

On the drive home, I became terrified, thinking that things could actually get worse than they already were. There was a small part of me that was proud of making it through another public experience, however. And yet another part of me that wanted to challenge all this bullshit and win at the end. *I lost everything? Bring it on. I have bipolar disorder? Bring it on. I have brain cancer? Bring it on.* The positive moment passed, and I went back to being terribly anxious and afraid.

AN ATTEMPT

The neurological exam came out negative, and I was back to living my life, mainly worried about bipolar disorder without the threat of some other form of doom on top of it. I was particularly reflective one day while doing the puzzle, becoming slightly more aware of the small progress that had been made in my recovery since returning home. My mind was on autopilot. *There's like one hundred different shades of blue in this puzzle.* A bird chirped, and I took a deep breath. *Okay, that chirp is probably not important.* I got a hit of anxiety and a nervous laugh came out. *Okay, so I couldn't focus on anything when I first came home.* I connected two blue pieces. *I still have no clue what meds I'm taking or how they work, but I know that I have to take them, and it's not as bad as it was when I first started. They aren't going to kill me.*

"Brett? What are you doing?" my mom yelled down, interrupting my train of thought.

"Puzzle! What else would I possibly be doing? My life sucks!" I had to throw in some drama to remind myself that bipolar had taken my life away, and I was never getting better, no matter what my thoughts were telling me. At least I could control the self-induced negative thoughts. *I deserve this.*

I thought about overcoming my fear of getting blood work, going out to eat, and keeping my composure when I thought things were about to escalate at the neurological exam. *So what's the big deal?* But it was a big deal. I had performed important actions and slightly moved the needle toward recovery without realizing it.

The same could be said about how my mom was supporting me. I appreciated her cooking and willingness to drop everything to make sure I was okay, but I became furious and annoyed at petty things like her being on her phone while in midconversation. My reactions were over the top as I projected my frustration with my situation onto her.

If I had not been so frustrated with my mom, then I would not have had the urge to find new people to spend time with. I hadn't used my phone very often since coming home, mainly because I was still convinced that chemical waves were being transferred from the screen directly into my brain, giving me scary but special powers. I thought about Dr. E. *Is it useful? I don't know. Having the powers themselves would be useful. I'll have to ask him.* I took a quick note in my phone for the next session: "Is collecting signals from my phone to make me more powerful useful or not? I really didn't know."

After a few more annoying altercations with my mom, I had no choice but to go through my phone and find a friend. I was receiving daily calls from my younger brother, Russel, who lived in Chicago, and occasional check-ins from my older brother, Jerry, from Philadelphia; but I was in need of human interaction that was closer to home and not my mother. My mind threw abstract darts at me that were as painful as real darts as I scrolled through the contact list. *Noah, cooler than me. No. Bill, probably making a lot of money and wouldn't care. No. Oliver, probably has a family by now. No.* I played this out for a bunch of contacts before coming across Sierra.

Sierra and I had met years ago while working at a local gym after my second recovery. She was working the front desk when I walked in for my first day and was the most beautiful woman I had ever seen. I felt an instant attraction to her. I was very focused on doing well at my job and didn't go out of my way to get to know her until a few weeks in. We hit it off over a game of Words with Friends and started to spend more time together. We had a playful banter at work and would go out downtown for drinks and dancing. We dated off and on over the next few years, and she even made a trip to visit me when I first moved to Texas. Unfortunately, the timing was never right, and we lost touch when I entered into a new relationship a year later in Texas. I had no idea what she was up to or if she would even respond, but for some reason, she was the only one I felt comfortable reaching out to at this time. I still felt vulnerable and anxious, more about how she would think of my new situation and lack of independence. *Oh, hey, Sierra, I live with my mom now and don't work! Ugh.*

Then I heard my mom's voice. "Brett? What are you doing up there?"

"Nothing!" I yelled back. *I have to do this.* I sent a text to Sierra and put my phone away. *Okay, back to the puzzle.*

BIOFEEDBACK

Sierra responded, thankfully, and we began texting, but it did not remove the anxiety I felt about socializing. The few times that I had been out of the house and around other people since I came home were very uncomfortable, a combination of light-headedness, fear, hallucinations, and anxiety. While I was getting more reps dealing with these hard things, they did not seem to be getting easier. I was very good at forecasting what was going to happen if I was ever out with my friends. *Hey, Brett, long time no see. What brought you home? Why are you acting so funny? Why do you have to be home so early? Why don't you want to drink? You always had before. Do you have an issue with alcohol? Are you an alcoholic? What are you doing now?* The hell-like buzz would return as I struggled to come up with answers to these made-up questions.

I reported everything I could to Dr. D, but the right cocktail of medication was still not figured out. My mom was heavily focused on getting second and third opinions and was displeased with the level of service. "He sees Brett for only fifteen minutes once a month!" she would yell into the phone to whoever was listening on the other end. I wasn't interested in changing doctors and meeting new people, but she did have a point. I was finding much value in my sessions with Dr. E, so I brought these social issues to him.

"Have a seat, Brett," Dr. E said as he opened the door. I had become more comfortable on the maroon couch, so that's where I sat. He picked up his weapon and notepad and asked, "So what's going on?"

Bio-feedback

"Well, I texted a friend and might hang out with her soon, but it's coming with an outpouring of fear and anxiety when I think about my social life."

"It's great that you made a connection. Why do you think it's coming with fear and anxiety?"

"Well, I picture a conversation with friends out in public, the questions they will ask me, the answers that I will give." My heart began to race. "I don't feel so well." My breathing became heavier, and I felt panic coming from my stomach. "I can't breathe." I had a flashback to the hospital experience a short time ago where I lost the use of my left hand during a devastating panic attack. The room became fuzzy, but I could still hear his voice.

"Brett, take a deep breath and place two fingers on your wrist."

I followed his orders and felt my heart beating. *Okay, I'm still alive.*

"Now continue to take deep breaths and focus on your pulse."

I followed his orders again. *Okay, I'm feeling better.* And then I came out of the panic attack.

"Brett, what you just did there was use biofeedback to help yourself recover from the panic attack."

Good to know. I took a few more deep breaths, and we got back into the session. I felt fine. *Okay, so a panic attack is just that, panic. But it will pass if I go into biofeedback mode, and I will be fine after.* A connection was made that I could add to my tool kit in case of future attacks.

We continued our discussion like I had not just had a near-death experience because I didn't. "I care what my friends will think of me. Part of me just wants to come out and say that I have bipolar disorder before we even start the conversation."

"Brett, you are free to share with people whatever you like. Over time, you'll have a better understanding of where the boundary is."

"Okay. Well, how about I just make the boundary with anyone outside of family. Family can know. Everyone else cannot."

"I can see why that would make it easier for you, and you can experiment with that if you like. You might find that it's not so black and white, but that is your discovery to make."

I'm so confused. "Okay, that makes sense," I said.

During the timid, slow drive home, I had more time to think. *No progress made on that session. What a waste of time.* I called my mom.

"Hey, Brett, are you sure you can call me while driving?"

"Yes, Mom."

"How was therapy?"

"Therapy sucked, just like my life."

"Did you tell him about the puzzle?"

No, I had a panic attack and have no clue how I'm ever going to interact with my friends for the rest of my life. "Yes, Mom."

When I got home, I felt really sad and depressed. I did plan on facing my fear and asking to hang out with Sierra, but it didn't change anything. And even if I did complete the task, there were so many more that would be too difficult for me. I ordered a pizza and felt comfort. Pizza tasted the same both before and after I was diagnosed with bipolar disorder.

KAREN'S CAR

All five of us are at the dinner table laughing, telling stories, and eating pounds of homemade brisket. The dogs are in on the fun, guilting us into feeding them under the table. I take a second to breathe it all in. This is what life is all about. My dad pushes his chair back and stands up. He takes one step and falls through the floor, leaving the four of us confused and worried. My mom stands up, and she falls, followed by both of my brothers. I'm left alone at the table. I'm afraid to stand up, so I sit and wait. Wait for something to happen. I'm sweating and afraid.

"Brett! Your dad is on the phone!" I sit up from the couch and feel a sense of relief, but then, I am reminded that my reality is not so much better than that nightmare I just had.

"Hey, bud, how are you?"

Bud? I thought about what I really wanted to tell him. *I'm not doing so well. I'm scared. I don't think I can do this.* "I'm fine," I said.

"Good," he replied. "You should really start thinking about what kind of work you want to do. It will help you not think of yourself so much while you recover."

"Uh, okay." I felt anxious thinking about my current social issues, and then adding work to the mix made it worse.

"Also, Karen has offered to let you use her car." Karen was my stepmom. I thought about how timid I was behind the wheel driving my mom's car but saw the value in having something that moved the needle slightly to making me more independent.

"That's very nice of her."

"Yes, it is. I'll come by, and we can get it together."

"Okay." I hung up the phone. "Mom! Dad is coming over and is letting me use Karen's car for a while."

She accommodated the request as usual, not stepping on anyone's toes and allowing her ex-husband to come and go as he pleased.

My dad was someone that I had always looked up to and wanted to earn respect from until he left my mom during my freshman year of college. That was ten years ago, but our issues were never resolved. Our relationship had formed into a weird mesh of confusion, anger, and frustration on my end, and an I'm-doing-everything-I-can mindset on his side. It was a very complex situation, especially when you added my mom and two brothers, whom I was very close with, into the mix because they all had their own set of issues. I knew that he loved me, but I felt awkward when he was around. He walked in like he was picking me up to take me to school. I rode shotgun for the hour-long drive to the garage where Karen's car was waiting. When he turned the key in the ignition, classic rock blasted from the speakers. *Surely, he's going to turn that down.* After a few more seconds, I asked politely, "Can you turn that down?"

He turned it down immediately. "Yes, of course. Sorry."

He cares. He's just clueless to my current situation. He began breaking down my situation as if it were like any other hard event that one went through. "It's a tough thing you have going on here. It will get better with time. I've been there. I know what you are going through."

"I know, I know." I acted tough on the outside, but I felt worthless internally. I had nothing to report that would make him proud. Everything that I might say would have sounded stupid. *Did you know I'm working on a big puzzle? Did you know I drove all by myself for the first time the other day? Did you know I finally reached out to a friend?* None of that was good enough.

We made it to the garage, and my dad left me alone in the car. I had just enough time to start seeing faces in the clouds and scary men in the woods. Then an old Honda rolled out of the garage.

"Karen has had this car for a while, but it's safe. Hop in and follow me home."

My dad hustled over to his car, and I hopped in Karen's, noticing the roll-up windows and the odometer reading a number that was over one hundred thousand. I didn't even have my seat belt on yet when my dad started to move. He made a difficult left out of the lot, and I had to wait to let a car pass. *He's gonna think I'm a bad driver.* I became anxious but finally caught up. He eventually slowed to let his disabled son stay close behind him. He led me to a nearby diner where similar thoughts and feelings continued. I mainly listened to stories going on in his life. When we finally made it back to my mom's, she looked at the old car with concern.

"Brett's gotta pick up the pace a little bit," he teased and meant no harm.

Ha ha ha! So funny. I'm such a loser.

Although I was beat-up emotionally on the trip to pick up Karen's car, the end result was that I had Karen's car. It would make it easier to try new things without needing to take my mom's car. Sierra and I continued to chat, and she informed me that her house was only ten minutes away from my mom's house. *Very convenient. Going to be hard to make excuses.* I knew that my first trip out of the house for a social interaction would be in Karen's old car to Sierra's house.

LIGHT CONNECTION

I felt a nervous buzz the next morning while typing out a text to Sierra that I would hang out at her house that afternoon. *This could be fun. I miss Sierra.* I hit the send button and became worried. *What am I doing! I'm not myself. This is going to suck.* I escalated the situation by thinking of the big picture. *It's ridiculous that I can't even go to a friend's house without my whole world shifting! I'm never going to be the same. My life sucks.* I looked at myself in the mirror and took note of how normal my face looked, even with the shouting match going on behind the curtains. I smirked. *I'm going to go. It will be fine. I'm not going to go. I'm going to cancel.* I justified changing my decision every minute or so. Finally, I decided to hit the puzzle to take the edge off. *Since when did I become so indecisive?*

I got lost in the puzzle for most of the morning and left myself an hour to prepare for my visit with Sierra. *Okay, I took my meds this morning, check. I ate breakfast this morning, check. I took my meds this afternoon, check. I ate lunch this afternoon, check.* Through all the painful experiences after being diagnosed, my brain was learning to check itself and ensure I was doing the healthy tasks necessary for my survival. *Drink a bunch of water.* I chugged some water. I looked around, prepared, but still with forty-five minutes to kill. I went back to the puzzle. *I can do this. It's just seeing an old friend. You know she won't judge you. It's close by. You can drive. You can handle this.* My clearest thoughts typically came while scanning the five-thousand-piece puzzle that seemingly had no end.

The positive self-talk had me ready to go, ready to do what was necessary to meet my friend, and ready to say "fuck you" to bipolar disorder. *I know I can do this.* My body was treating this event like a mini Super Bowl, and I was ready. I wasn't pleased with the level of effort it took to get to this place, but I was ready for this step and didn't need anyone's approval to understand what it meant to me.

I got in the car and drove quietly to Sierra's house. I was feeling confident and turned the radio on. *Turn around! Turn around!* The disc jockey didn't believe that I could have a successful trip.

Is that real? Probably not, but maybe? I was a bit rattled after getting feedback from the radio that I should turn back. It did, after all, take every ounce of my positive energy to get in this headspace and make the trip in the first place.

I pulled up to her small house and knocked on the door.

"Hey, Brett!" she said as she smiled and let me in.

"Hey," I said back.

Her two cats swarmed me, and she instantly put them in the basement, remembering that I was allergic. "Sorry about that, Brett. Want anything to drink?"

"No, I'm fine," I said.

Shit, always say yes to water. "Can I use your bathroom real quick?"

"Yes, it's right upstairs."

I took my shoes off to be polite and made it to the bathroom, where I chugged out of the sink after missing my opportunity when she asked. *I'll be using a lot of peoples' bathrooms the way I drink water now.* I made eye contact with myself in the mirror on the way out. *So far so good.*

I came back downstairs, and we caught up while standing in her kitchen. I must have come off pretty normal because she didn't seem to be shy about sharing things going on in her life. As she talked, I became a bit light-headed and had to lean against the counter, still nodding and appearing to be interested in her every word. A few minutes later, I could feel panic bubbling up through my throat.

"Can we sit down?" I asked.

"Sure," she said, "everything okay?"

"Yeah, I just got a bit dizzy."

I used the biofeedback method from Dr. E and settled myself down by slyly checking my pulse while still engaged in conversation.

"So what's going on with you?" she asked. Sierra was never the type to pry, but she was interested in my life. I felt comfortable.

"Well." I slowed down a bit and got slightly emotional. "I was diagnosed with bipolar disorder. I'm really off and not feeling like myself." *And then some.* She was supportive.

"Well, you still look good to me."

"I don't seem off to you at all?" I asked.

"Not really."

"Oh."

Sierra and I watched a show or two on Hulu, and then I felt an urge to get out of there and recalibrate after this novel experience. On the drive home, I had new thoughts to address. *She couldn't tell anything was different about me? She was just being nice. Anyone who knew me before would clearly see how sad and weird I am now.* I took one look at the radio dial and felt anxious. *The radio never used to scare me.*

MEDS

Everything was still terrible. I had been home for a few months living with my mom, without a job, struggling to do the most basic tasks, and taking pills that I didn't understand. The small wins like getting a full night's sleep, driving, and meeting up with Sierra were overshadowed by the bipolar diagnosis and the real fact that my life sucked now. *What can I do today? What can I do today? What can I do today!* The puzzle looked boring. *What can I do today? What can I do today? What can I do today!* Turning on the TV was too scary. *What can I do today? What can I do today? What can I do today!* Reading was too hard.

Dr. D told me that the medication took time to work correctly and that he had seen slight progress during our short sessions. In my mind, I thought the pain and struggle that I was going through was part of living with bipolar and part of my life forever now. Somewhere in the throes of the nightmare of being in the middle of needing to do something but being too anxious and scared to do it, my attention gravitated toward my medication. I tried to stop passively listening and started to take a stronger interest in the chemicals that I was putting into my body three times a day.

I took a look at the collection of pill bottles perfectly organized on the kitchen counter. *Thanks, Mom!* I scoffed, feeling like nothing she could do was good enough. *Okay, let's play doctor.* I put all the bottles on my left and picked up one, reading the label. *I should just down all these.* "Zyprexa," it read.

I heard Dr. D's voice, *Zyprexa is an antipsychotic. We'll try it for a while.*

I wasn't currently on Zyprexa, which explained why there were only a few pills in the bottle. I moved the bottle to the right. *Next!* I pictured waiting at the DMV and my pill bottles were waiting in line miserably for me to address them. Risperdal. *Hello, my old friend.* Risperdal helped clear up my psychotic thoughts in my previous two episodes. Dr. D switched out Zyprexa for Risperdal because of its past success. *I should just down all these.* I took out one and a half pills, placed it on the counter, and moved the bottle to the safe zone with the Zyprexa. Lexapro. *Good to see you again, Lex.* I was having a little party with my medicine. Lexapro is an antidepressant. It, too, played a role in my previous two recoveries, which had been successful. It made sense to me why Dr. D would have me on both the Lexapro and Risperdal. *But I didn't have bipolar back then. WTF?* I took one and a half Lexapro pills out and added it to the group. *Next up!* Lithium. Doctors talked about lithium like it was placed on this earth by God himself. Dr. D called it "the gold standard" for treating bipolar disorder. He also explained that nobody knew how it worked and was discovered by accident, which was interesting for doctors but scary as hell for patients. *I should just down all these.* I took out four lithium pills. *Lithium is here to save the day!* I only went by the number of pills and wasn't aware of the actual milligram amounts. Apparently, that could change even if the pill looked the same. *Last but not least, Ativan!* Ativan felt nice, working like alcohol and calming my nerves. I added two Ativan to the mix.

I looked at the pills, noticing the different shapes, sizes, and purpose. *It's like Halloween! All these drugs, and I still feel like shit! The only one that feels like it's helping is Ativan. I'm still feeling depressed, feeling anxious, and seeing and hearing things that aren't there. I'm sluggish, stiff, hungry, nauseous, and tired.* I had a thought to not take the medicine. *That would be dumb. "One hundred percent of bipolar individuals who do not take their meds will have future episodes." That's pretty black and white.* So I swallowed my pride and all the pills individually, like an amateur.

My mom had been persistent about me telling Dr. D everything, a little too persistent. After every appointment, she would aggressively question me. "Did you tell him about your psychotic thoughts?" she'd ask.

"No, we just stared at each other for the whole appointment," I responded sarcastically. "And then I reported on how many bowel movements I had."

"Brett, give me a break."

I would always share what I thought to be important info with her. "Mom, I'm not sure the medicine is working."

"Did you tell him?" she asked.

I hadn't had the courage until our next appointment.

NEEDING CONTROL

"Hello, Brett, how are you feeling?" Dr. D asked.

I heard my mom's voice echoing inside my head. *Did you tell him this? Did you tell him that? Tell him everything!*

"I'm doing okay, but I need to report a few things." For some reason, I felt bad inside, like I was letting him down. *Your master plan isn't working too well, buddy.* "I'm still having psychotic thoughts, but not all the time." *And I know that some are still real, but you wouldn't understand.* I noticed a traffic light change from red to green out of his window, which served as confirmation that something bigger was still going on. "My muscles are achy, I'm still feeling very depressed, I worry about my kidneys, and I still feel anxious most of the day."

"Are these things that are getting worse or have they always been this way?" he asked.

"I don't know, but they feel worse."

He studied his notes for a few seconds and then reminded me, "The Risperdal was prescribed to help with the psychotic thoughts, and that's probably where the muscle achiness is coming from. The lithium can have an effect on your kidneys, so we should get another blood level."

Ugh, back to the phlebotomist.

"Lexapro is supposed to help with depression and your compulsive thinking, so I'm not sure what I'd like to do about that yet. Ativan is meant to relieve anxiety, so we may need to increase it." The rationale behind his decision to keep the Risperdal where it was, get a blood level, and raise the Ativan made sense to me. "And take the Ativan as needed. When you are feeling anxious, take the Ativan."

"Got it."

My mom was waiting for me in the kitchen when I returned home from the appointment. She gave me a warm hug. "I'm so proud of how you are handling all that you are going through."

"Thanks, Mom."

"How was the appointment?"

Here we go. "It went well. I just stopped by the pharmacy and got a few things. I also have to get blood work again."

"The pharmacy? Did he change something? Do you want me to call him?" she asked with concern.

"No, I'm fine." *Please don't make me explain all this to you right now.*

"Okay, but why the blood work? Will you please tell me what you two discussed?"

I sighed. "He gave me the option to take more Ativan when I'm anxious. He wanted to check my blood levels."

"Why?"

I sighed again. "I'm feeling more anxious than I'm putting on, and something in my stomach felt sore. I told him my kidney's hurt, and he wanted to check."

"What's making you anxious?"

Right now, it's you. "The same stuff we've been talking about, nothing new, just feeling more anxious. Might be because I'm doing more, and new things seem hard."

"Your blood levels might be off?"

"Yeah, they told us this in the beginning. Blood work is going to be a regular part of this."

She gave me another hug. "You're doing so well. You're so strong."

I patted her on the back and squirmed away. "It's just so weird to be on all this medication. Are you sure some of those stories I told you couldn't have happened? Like don't the backs of cars and outlets look like faces? Don't birds come and go, communicating with people in some way? Is it possible that a red streetlight might mean danger?"

"Brett, some of those things are true, but I don't see them as having as much meaning as you do."

"Are you really sure?"

"Yes, Brett." She gave me another hug.

I took a little extra Ativan over the next few days and felt buzzed, like when I used to drink alcohol before this whole bipolar mess. My psychotic thoughts came back stronger, and it was clear that the Ativan was calming me down physically but ramping up false thoughts. I called Dr. D.

"Okay, Brett, go back to where we were before with the Ativan."

I followed his orders but then couldn't sleep at night because my tolerance had risen. My mind was a scale without equal weight on each side.

On the next visit to Dr. D, I was out of whack, not getting good sleep but still having psychotic thoughts from all the medicine changes.

"Hello, Brett, I have good news. Your blood work is all good. How is everything else?"

"I'm not doing so well. This Ativan is really messing with me. I want to be on the least amount possible so I don't need to rely on it."

"Okay, Brett, well, it is as needed, so you can manage it however you like."

"Well, I take three or four pills per day. Can I just stop taking it?"

"Good question, Brett. No. We'll wean you off it. Stay on three for a few days, then two, then one. We'll talk before you stop completely. Sound good?"

"Yes, sounds good." On the drive home, I was fixated on getting off the Ativan. *You said you are gonna wean off the Ativan. No one told you, you had to do it. Do what you said you are going to do.* "I'm going to do it. I'm going to get myself off the Ativan," I said out loud, alone in the driver's seat, with both hands on the wheel.

THE GOOD AND THE BAD

My eyes gently opened, and the hell-like buzz of anxiety was not there. *That's nice.* I took a deep breath and felt the warm air moving in and out of my mouth. I noticed my stomach moving automatically up and down. I was a bit skeptical of these new pleasant feelings that I had not experienced in months, but I remained positive. I took a step out of bed. *One small step for me, one giant leap for me with bipolar disorder.* I took a few more leaps to the bathroom and got a good look at myself. *All right, not so bad.* I brushed my teeth with toothpaste and took a hot shower, feeling even better about today.

I was guided downstairs to the kitchen where I threw a few eggs in the pot and worked on the puzzle while waiting for the eggs to boil. I was intrigued by the puzzle. *Good morning, old friend.* There was a note on the counter with a picture of a heart. "Out getting coffee. Be back soon." I cracked the eggs and had a banana with a glass of water for breakfast. I gave the puzzle a break while eating and noticed an open newspaper within my reach. *Okay, take your time and focus.*

I set a goal for myself to read the short sections on the front page. *If you are able to take an interest in any of the sections, then finish the full article.* I felt nervous anxiety before diving in, not to be confused with the hell-like buzz. I took a few deep breaths and got through the first few sentences, then I finished the first section. *Oh, I can definitely still do this.* I felt excited, thinking about how my world would expand if I could focus enough to read and understand. I could have stopped there, but I had set a bigger goal, a goal to read the entire front page. I moved to the next section and felt the rumbling of the garage. I felt a weird panicky feeling that I had to speed up and finish before my mom made it upstairs with the coffee. I went a little bit faster, still absorbing the info. *Doesn't matter if she's here or not. Achieve your goal.* I continued.

"Good morning, Brett! I got you decaf," she said innocently.

"Thanks," I replied with my head down, using all my might to stay focused on reading.

"What are you reading?" she asked.

"Nothing," I mumbled, feeling more anxiety.

"Can I tell you a quick story?" she asked.

"Sure," I replied with my head still down, staring at the paper and no longer able to concentrate.

"I ran into Mrs. Johnson at the coffee place. Remember her son?"

"No." I was done with the paper, a bit irritated now, and was moving toward the pill bottles. *Take a deep breath. No reason you shouldn't be able to listen to this story while taking your meds.*

"She said he knew you." I rubbed shoulders with her to get to the medicine corner.

"Oh really?" I responded, only concerned with taking the right dosage.

"Yeah, are you sure you don't remember him?"

Okay Risperdal, Lexapro, lithium, Ativan, Zyprexa. I fumbled through the bottles and pulled my morning drugs from the group. "No," I replied with half of my focus.

"Do you think he might have been in Jerry's grade?"

Okay, pills are laid out. I'm going to pass on the Ativan this morning. I'll see how that goes. "No clue."

"Hmm, well, maybe it was Russel then?"

"Yeah, maybe," I said while filling up a glass of water and downing the pills.

She stared at me while doing it. "I'm still so amazed how you do that," she said.

"Thanks."

I was on a roll today and decided to lace up my shoes and attempt to go for a run because the puzzle was there for me all afternoon. I stepped outside into the cold and started jogging. *Make it around the whole complex and back.* My breathing became heavy instantly, and my legs started to hurt. Not only had I not jogged in a while, but I was barely moving during the day at all. *Come on, take the pain. Keep going. Just quit. It will be easier.* I decided to quit instantly, after only a few strides. *I suck.*

I came back inside. "Brett, weren't you going for a run? What happened?" she asked.

"Don't worry about it!" I said forcefully and slammed my feet up the stairs and sat on my bed, ripping my laces off my running shoes. *This is bullshit, getting all happy about reading a sentence or two, you disabled loser. You can't even run one-tenth of a mile. What a joke!* I became restless and anxious, not having anywhere to put this excess energy. I came downstairs and took the decaf off the counter. "Thanks for the decaf, Mom!" I said sarcastically as I slammed it down, spilling some. "Maybe someday I'll be able to have caffeine again like every other fucking person I know!" I started on the puzzle again, and she let me work in peace.

NEW ENVIRONMENTS

Crack! Sixteen heavy globes of different colors and designs smacked into one another and rolled across a flat green field. High walls in a rectangular shape fenced the worlds in; and deep, dark pitfalls were planted in every corner. While looking down on this universe, I wondered how many people were occupying each planet and how I could help them. I saw the yellow sun and the white moon. I saw a fiery red ball fall into one of the corner pockets, never to be seen again.

"Nice shot, Brett!" said my mom.

I blinked a few times and remembered where I was, the local pool hall.

The players on the other tables were managing their universes in a similar way but looking over at mine and trying to copy. I felt scared and anxious.

How did he drop the devil but keep the sun and the moon? a man with a biker vest and beard said to his friend from across the room.

I don't know. It just happened. Maybe it's because I'm special. I eyed up my next shot, which was a green world that had the number 6 on it. *It's 666. Put it where you put the devil.* The whole room was watching to see if I could defeat the devil and his goons. My shot went in, and the rest of the room went back to playing at their own tables. *That's right, assholes.*

"You are really on a roll, Brett!" said my mom.

I felt a buzz and knocked down a few more shots, checking the room after each one to make sure my enemies were in check. I missed my next shot and felt like I had let the whole world down. My mom lined up her shot and missed quickly. "Oh well," she said.

After pool, we walked next door for some thai food where the front desk girl, waitress, and everyone in the restaurant were evaluating my pool performance and making fun of how I thought I was changing the universe with my pool stick. I took the punches and ate lunch, not really sure how to describe what I was going through to my mom. I had time to reflect on the afternoon when I got home. I went back and forth. *It was a big step to go out to play pool like that and then have a meal afterward. Two activities back-to-back. I've never done that. Two activities back-to-back? So what? You are twenty-nine, and that's a big deal?* I leaned on the latter thought being the more accurate of the two.

Every time I made a bit of progress, I reminded myself that it wasn't good enough. *This is such bullshit. I need to do something to show that I'm normal! What should I do?* Nothing came to me. *You're pathetic. Congrats on making a couple shots in pool and eating lunch. Congrats!* Being alone with my thoughts was torturous and never ending. Even if I was with my mom, I still felt alone with my thoughts.

"Brett! Russel is calling and wants to talk. Are you up for it?" my mom called down from upstairs.

"Yeah," I hadn't paid close attention to my phone since I came back, so she ran down and handed me hers. "Hey, Russel."

"Hey, B, how are you?"

"Ehh, I'm fine. I played some pool with mom today."

"That doesn't sound so bad. I'm sure it's been hard."

"Yeah, it's been hard."

"All right, well, I'm going to call you every day to check in. Love you."

"Love you too." *Nice of him to call.*

After I explained to my mom how my call with Russell went, I had more time alone with my thoughts. *Dude, fucking put the TV on and sit there. It's fine.* I put on Ray Donovan and made myself comfortable on the couch. I took a few deep breaths and noticed how my mind would navigate delusional thoughts versus clear thoughts.

A gun went off in the show, and I felt anxiety. *Am I being abstractly shot? No.* The anxiety passed.

Ray said, *I'm going to the bar.*

Is he telling me to go to the bar? No. Is he making fun of me for not being able to drink? Maybe. No, probably not.

Ray made eye contact with me. *I said I'm going to the bar.*

Well, maybe?

Ray continued, *Brett, I'm going to the bar, and you can't go to the bar. You'll never go to the bar again. You are weak.*

This is ridiculous. I turned off the TV and put the remote down aggressively. *I guess I still can't watch TV.*

THE AVIARY

The restlessness was what pushed me to say yes when my mom asked me to go to the aviary. I had decided that feeling embarrassed, vulnerable, scared, and anxious was better than feeling embarrassed, vulnerable, scared, anxious, and restless. *Pick your poison.*

It was important to mentally prepare before leaving the safety of my house. *Okay, this is going to suck, but everything sucks.* I first thought logically about where my body would have to go physically to get out today, regardless of what my mind was telling me to do. *Literally, just get dressed, get in the car, sit, stand, walk through the aviary with a bunch of birds and people annoying you, and get back to the car. You can do this. Keep it simple.*

My bedroom became a locker room as I got dressed. *Let's go. We can do this.* I made it to the car, not paying close attention to what my mom was doing or saying. I sat in the car on the thirty-minute drive, staring out of the window and feeling free and trapped at the same time. We found a parking spot, and I took one more deep breath, seeing the building in the distance. *Deep breath. Let's go. You can do this.* My mom and I didn't sprint into the aviary like a football team coming out of the tunnel, but we did walk slowly and under control, a different type of positive energy.

In the lobby, there were children screaming and running around, an embarrassing reminder that these were now my peers. I scoffed, thinking about what my life had come to. *Walk and be annoyed by birds and people, remember? That's this part.* I took a deep breath and let my mom lead. She was aware that I was not all there but allowed me some free space without asking if I was okay every few minutes.

Then she observed me start to panic, get very upset, and run away from the aviary.

Then we were back at home, sitting across from each other at the dining room table with the puzzle separating us.

"Brett, are you willing to explain to me what happened back there? Did I do something. I feel lucky that you came back and apologized."

Finally, someone asked something other than "How are you?"

I grabbed a piece of paper and pen. "Basically, here's me, here's you, and here's all the people at the aviary." I drew a picture for her. "They're all having conversations with each other. Here's a family of two, three, whatever." I scribbled a bit more, pointing out the people. "They are all having experiences, and so are we. It feels like everything they are seeing and doing is some kind of test. Everything they say, I can hear it as though it relates to me, you, and both of us. Here's an example." I scribbled a bit more. "Here's me, you, the eagle, and people while we were sitting on the bench looking at the birds. The dad with his kid says, 'Look at its wings!' I take that as 'Look at my wings, my arms.' 'Look at their eyes. Their eyes are so beautiful,' he might say. I take that as 'Both of us have beautiful eyes,' and he's talking about us. A kid will yell, 'Stop!' And in my brain, that is like, 'Stop doing this thing where you read other people's thoughts!'" My mom laughed nervously. "Then the bird will fly, and something will shine and reflect off the floor. I'll hear 'Did they catch that ball at the baseball game?' I only hear the 'Did they catch that' part, and I'll think they are saying, 'Did they catch that glare on the ground?'"

This is the world that I experience in my head.

"So the whole time you were sitting watching the eagle, you were doing this as well? Did you like the eagle?" my mom asked.

"I realized if I stare at something in motion, then I can focus, but something still forces me to think about other things. That's part of what happened today. That's what I can describe. Even in a restaurant, even as we're walking, even the fucking Waze computer voice can sound like *smile* instead of 'mile'. I have developed a side of this where I just need to trust that things are okay. They are the way they are, even if I'm perceiving all these things. The more that I trust, nothing happens. The more I freak out, the harder it is."

"So we need to try more things," she added.

"Yes, but at a certain point, it's boring. Like, why does going to the aviary have to be such a big deal?"

THE GYM

I was in a hoodie and sweatpants early in the morning, lying on the couch with the remote in my hand. *Let's just see what's on TV.* I carefully hit the power button, knowing that anything was possible once it came on. The screen remained black for a second after the audio started.

Well, guys, let's recap what he's doing.

The screen came on, and three new reporters made eye contact with me, still chatting. *When he first got the news, it was funny to watch him squirm. He really was like a child that needed his parents,* said the lead.

The blonde on his right chimed in, *I couldn't agree more. He's calling it a "hell-like buzz," but isn't that a little dramatic? I mean, he's not in hell, is he?*

Then the other reporter defended me, *Have either of you two ever gone through what he's going through? That's what I thought.*

I took a deep breath and digested what I just heard. *Just listen to what they say without judgment.* I didn't respond or react, just kept breathing and letting the anxiety pass.

Guys, he seems pretty spoiled, complaining about living with his mom. Anyone would be lucky to have her around.

Yeah, but what about the restlessness? That looks terrible. Imagine a bug crawling around inside of you all day!

Yeah! I agreed with the reporter and then took a deep breath. *That's just a reporter on the TV. She's not cheering you on.* I got more anxious but took another deep breath.

The next few minutes was a ping-pong match of reality versus delusion in my head with the TV being the playing field. *Delusion feels real and makes me believe it. Reality sets in, and I'm skeptical. Delusion feels real and makes me believe it. Reality sets in, and I'm skeptical. Repeat.* It was exhausting and frustrating. For some reason, it was important to me to watch the show all the way through, like some sort of gauge of how I was doing compared to the last time I tried to watch TV. *Couldn't get through Ray Donovan. Got through the news, though!*

Even though I was not thinking clearly, I was still developing good habits like going to the gym. I had a nightmare experience on the stepper the first time at the gym but got a little more comfortable on the cardio equipment. Today, I decided I was going to try weights. One benefit of being unemployed with a chronic disability was that the free weight area wouldn't be as crowded in the middle of the day. I mentally prepared for this like the aviary, even though that didn't turn out so well. *Get in your car, drive there, park your car, check in, lift some fucking weights, leave.* I was focused and made it to the lift-some-fucking-weights part of the task list. On the way over to the free weight area, I noticed the closed caption on the TV read, *He's so weak now.*

I'm fucking weak now? Shut the fuck up! I don't give a fuck if that's real or not real. I was finally pumped up and pissed off in the right environment. I knocked out a full-body workout that rivaled how my workouts used to be. I was aware that I didn't have any psychotic thoughts when I was pushing my body physically and feeling the pain of lifting weights.

I kept the heaven-like buzz going and ran two miles on the treadmill, feeling no pain. *There we go.* I clapped for myself mentally and walked comfortably out of the gym and into my car. I drove back to the house, opened the door, and smelled an amazing meal that my mom had made.

"Looking good!" she said.

I went upstairs and took a hot shower. I threw on the hoodie and sweatpants that I had started my day with and had a nice meal with my mom.

I was exhausted from the workout and skipped the Ativan before bed. *I only took one today.* I felt good about weaning off it myself like I said I was going to. I hit the pillow. *Wow, that was a great workout. Okay, time for bed.* I lay there for a few minutes. *Why am I not sleeping?* I tossed and turned for the next hour or so and then became frustrated. *This day really wasn't that good. I've got news reporters talking about me through the TV and closed caption. I've got a workout that apparently didn't make me tired. I had a good meal, but God only knows how much butter was in the mashed potatoes. I'm fat. It was really only one workout. I must have gotten lucky. Fuck this.* I got up, took an Ativan, and was fast asleep in no time.

NEW IDEAS

"Does God exist?" I asked the most cliché question in the world to my spiritual advisor, The Rabbi. The Rabbi was referred by Dr. D and served as someone who I could talk to, to answer questions outside the wheelhouse of my doctor and therapist. I wasn't necessarily looking for answers, but I took interest in the conversations. I was raised Jewish and got my Bar Mitzvah at age thirteen but did not keep up with my studies and fell off over time. As an adult, I was still unsure what I believed in.

"Yes," the middle-aged Orthodox man replied across the table with no hesitation.

How could he possibly know that? If there was one thing that I had learned over those first few months of hard recovery was that it was okay to be blunt and speak my mind while talking to advisors that were here to help me. "How could you possibly know that?" I replied. He gave me a warm smile indicating that there was nothing I could say that would make him defensive.

"Brett, a rabbi was talking to an atheist and said, 'If you don't believe in God, then sell me your afterlife for twenty dollars.' The atheist wouldn't do it. 'One hundred dollars?' The atheist still wouldn't do it. 'Why?' the rabbi asked. 'I don't know.' The point of this story is that even those who don't believe still hold on to a deep-seated feeling that they cannot understand."

"Yeah, I get that. I'm still not so sure that is God, though."

"It takes time and faith. We study and pray to become close with God."

As I asked other difficult questions and he gave me answers that were worth thinking more about, I loosened my views slightly. *Even if I don't believe in God and that everything ends when I die, it makes me feel better to think that life goes beyond what happens on earth.* We then read a few sections from a digestible version of the *Tanya*, and he gave me a book to take with me and read called *Toward a Meaningful Life* by Simon Jacobson.

I always enjoyed my meetings with The Rabbi and left with a warm feeling that things were going on that were way bigger than me and my recovery. I did have to be careful, however, not to get too lost in thoughts about God and heaven because they both played a major, dangerous role in my manic episodes.

I'd drive home from my meeting with The Rabbi seeing things slightly differently. A cloud would shift. *Normal, God, or psychotic thought?* A light would turn from red to green. *Normal, God sending a message, or psychotic thought?* Ache in my stomach. *Normal bellyache, God punishing me, psychotic thought, or side effects of medicine?* My mind was living in the real world rotating between three different perspectives.

During my next doctor's appointment, it was reported that my blood levels were a little off and my mood was a bit down. It turned out that I had developed hypothyroidism from the lithium that I was taking, a common condition in which there was not enough thyroid hormone in the body. The solution to this was to meet with an endocrinologist and take a drug called Synthroid. For Synthroid to be effective, it must be taken without eating or drinking an hour before and after taking the drug.

My doctor casually mentioned, "Oh, you'll be on this for the rest of your life."

Add it to the pile of meds.

I was still struggling but had a lot of support from doctors and family. I was getting comfortable with these people. My mom and brother were convinced that Dr. D wasn't giving me proper attention because I was still hallucinating. Getting comfortable with hallucinating was not really progress. So they pulled their resources and got me registered for a more structured outpatient program at a downtown university. When I got there, I was interviewed by a few people, and they approved me for the program. They were very happy to have me, although I was skeptical and not sure if I wanted to be there. *This will be the college of recovery!*

When I lay in bed that night, I was anxious and not sure if I wanted to go to the program. I wasn't doing it for myself, I was doing it for my family. The next morning, I insisted on driving myself like an independent person. I walked into the facility that reminded me of the psychiatric hospital, took a deep breath, and entered a classroom full of empty chairs. I was the first one there and twenty minutes early.

RECOVERY CLASS

The chalkboard read, "Breathe in. Breathe out." *Good advice.* I slid into the armchair desk that was closest to the door and waited, feeling light-headed. I stared out of the window for a few minutes and observed the other desks floating in circles all around me. *Raising up the class already, heh.* Then a man about my age, casually dressed, walked in and sat right next to me. *There were like fifteen other options, dude!*

He said, "Hey."

And I said, "Hey." Then we both stared out of the window for a few minutes awkwardly. My anxiety started to build, and I glanced at the chalkboard. *Breathe in. Breathe out.*

We were about two minutes away from the start of the class, and it was still just the two of us. I pictured my old basketball coach forcefully reminding his team that "If you are early, then you are on time. If you are on time, then you are late. If you are late, then—" He'd make a face like he just smelled garbage. Over the next few minutes, my classmates started to pour in. There was an even balance of gender, a few older, a few younger, and a few of my age.

Many of these people already knew each other and were carrying notes from previous classes. I felt underprepared. *Oh shit, I'm already behind.* When the instructor walked in ten minutes late, I judged her harshly. *You are the one that's gonna save my life?* She handed me and my neighbor a new workbook.

"Just do the best you can to catch up today."

Catch up? I thought I was just starting today.

"Hey, everyone! How are we all doing today?"

The class was in good spirits, but I was feeling trapped. I kept a close eye on the door to my left in case I needed to escape. *Breathe in. Breathe out.*

"We're going to go around the room and see how we did on the homework. Oh, and before we get started, say hi to Brett and Mike." The class looked at us and I looked down. "Okay, let's start over here. Why don't you share, Bobby?"

Bobby was a teenager wearing baggy pants, an oversize shirt, and a goth chain. He had bad acne and messy hair. "Well, uhhh, well, uhhh, well, uhhh."

Okay, I'm not the only one with issues here.

"Well, uhh. I didn't take my medicine every day last week, but I did fill my time with leisurely video game time every day."

"Okay, Bobby, great job on finding your leisure activity, but we really gotta take our meds."

"I know, but it's really my doctor's fault. I'm going to talk to him today."

Huh, are you serious?

"Okay, Bobby, thanks for sharing."

Next was an older woman. "I'm having a great week! I completed my homework assignment of baking a cake!"

"That's great!" the instructor replied. "Anything else you want to share?"

"No, that was my one goal for the week, and I did it!"

Really? I judged her hard. Then the attention moved to a man my age.

"I'm having a shit week."

Finally, some honesty.

"I just had what I think they are calling a manic episode. I have no clue what's going on."

My hand went up in the air. *Why am I doing this?*

"Yes, Brett?" She looked at me like "What could you possibly have to say?"

"I've had three manic episodes. You'll be fine. Just listen to your doctors."

"That's good advice, Brett."

I felt good for a second before a nurse interrupted the class, "Brett?" I hopped up, remembering that I saw a new doctor here once a week. I went into his office, and the door closed behind me.

Is he kidding? Pump me full of as much lithium as possible? Cancel all my other doctors? Do it by the end of the week? I hustled out of his office and headed straight for the elevator. I paced until it came, rode it down, and walked out of the building without my classroom materials. I called my mom, "Mom, this isn't going to work for me."

"Why, what happened?"

"The doctor in there told me he's going to poison me. I'm not going back in."

"Did you already leave?"

"No, I'm standing outside."

"Brett, can you please give it another shot? We worked really hard to get you that spot."

I started walking to my car. "Mom, there is no way in hell I'm going back to that place, ever."

She sounded a little frustrated, but I made it home safe. I felt relieved, but everyone else felt stress because they had to go back to the drawing board and find me new doctors. I didn't mind staying with my current crew.

Over the next few days, the class instructor left multiple voice mails, trying to convince me to come back. I deleted them all.

MISSING OUT

Oh, this is bad, really bad. I was holding my phone, watching the messages come in. *How am I ever going to do this? It's too hard. They'll never understand.* I thought about the last few months and worried about the next few. *I have no idea how I'm going to feel. It's too much.* I didn't know what to say, so I didn't respond at all.

"Mom!"

"Yes, Brett!"

"Warren is getting married, and I'm invited to the bachelor party." I paced back and forth. "Fuck! I don't think I can go."

"When is it?"

"It's in a few months. My friends are all in town asking me to hang out."

"Well, Brett, why don't you just see how you feel in a few months then. Revisit it then."

"Yeah, but they are all hanging out tonight! What am I going to do?"

"You don't have to do anything, but you could give it a shot."

"Give it a shot? They will all be drinking and maybe smoking." *Wow, I really sound like a loser right now.*

"Well, it's still early. See how you feel later."

"Okay."

I held onto my phone and watched the messages roll by: "Can't wait to see you, fools!" "Warren is off the market!" "We're gonna rage!" *Not a chance in hell I'm going to this thing.* I was fairly certain that this wedding was not happening for me. I felt guilty and embarrassed that I wouldn't be able to attend one of my best friends' weddings. The least I could do was give Warren a call and explain the situation to him. I was anxious but reminded myself that my true friends would understand.

"Hello?"

"Hey, Warren! It's Brett."

"Stevens! Thanks for calling, man. Can't wait to see you."

"Yeah, congrats." I sounded fine but was unsure about how my words would come out. "Hey, Warren, I wanted to tell you that I won't be able to make it to the wedding and bachelor party. Did you know I was home from Texas?"

"Stevens, it's totally fine, man. Yeah, I heard something but didn't have any details."

"Do you remember what happened in the West Side when we were living with Aaron?"

"Yeah."

"So it pretty much happened again. Only this time, they diagnosed me with bipolar disorder."

I don't know if he was unsure of what he just heard, but he responded with "You'll be all right. Maybe you could see us tonight?"

I just wanna hide. I felt bad letting him down again. "Yeah, that's fine."

"Cool, see you soon, Stevens."

Why? Why, why, why? Why did I have to tell him I would hang out tonight? I was more anxious about tonight than anything I had done previously. There would be alcohol there, something that I was committed to giving up. I wasn't tempted by alcohol, but I feared the conversation about why I didn't drink anymore. *What will they think of me?* The torturous day dragged on, and I overcame my last chance to quit and not go to my friend's house.

When I opened the door, they were all already there and buzzed. Five of my closest friends lined up and hugged me one at a time, not treating me any differently than they always had. "Want a beer, Stevens?"

"No, I'm good."

"Okay, cool."

Well, that was that. I scoffed thinking about how many hours I had stressed about that conversation all day. I sat on the couch and let them do most of the talking all night. One of my friends suggested we play Uno, something we had never done as a group before. I hadn't realized until later that they chose that game for me. They knew I was a card shark and would excel and have fun without drinking.

The game of Uno was a major time killer during my stays at the three psychiatric hospital experiences that I had. It was bizarre to circle around with my best friends and play a game that I had also played with murderers, bipolars, and suicidal individuals. There was nothing else to do or think about as we played Uno. It felt like old times.

Around 9:00 p.m., my phone buzzed, reminding me that it was med time. The night was just beginning, and I had already needed to think about leaving. I felt anxious that I was out past nine o'clock and lost track of time for a few hours. I thought that this might be the recipe for another manic episode if I didn't get it together. I said my goodbyes and felt good about seeing my old friends, even though I'd miss the wedding. As always, there was an overpour of negative thoughts associated with the fact that I couldn't drink, couldn't stay out late, and was driving back to my mom's place. I refused to accept that giving up drinking and staying out late wasn't so bad.

DR. F

"Please, Brett, just see her," said my mom.

"No! I like the people I'm working with now and don't want to change," I replied.

"But I really think she can help you. She only has a few patients and has a much more systematic approach than your current providers."

"Do you remember what happened when you sent me to that outpatient program? I'm still traumatized."

"This will be different, Brett. It's one-on-one. I need you to see her."

"This isn't about what you need, though!" I roared back.

"It's right up the road!" she said and didn't back down.

For weeks, I resisted the idea of changing doctors, which led to arguments between my mom and me. I was comfortable with the actions that I needed to take to get to and from my current providers. Getting out of my comfort zone was not something I was prepared to do at a moment's notice, especially when it was my mom who was asking me to do it. We compromised. "As long as I get to keep Dr. E."

"Deal," she said.

My mom drove me to my first appointment with Dr. F. Her office was only ten minutes away from where we lived. I had a familiar feeling of anxiety as we parked in the public garage and walked into the waiting room. *Hey, I've been here before.* I realized that this was the same waiting room that I was in over a decade ago when I was being evaluated before going straight to the downtown psychiatric hospital. We had a seat in the waiting room, where the same classical music was playing.

I'm speeding on the highway down South, and I miss the exit to pick my brother up at the airport. I make a hard left and smash over the divider to get to the other side. Why did the chicken cross the road? To get to the other side. I opened my eyes and gave my mom a little smile. *I introduce myself to a tall man in the hospital, my roommate, and ask him what he's here for. He pulls his turtleneck down and exposes the bruises on his neck. "I tried to kill myself."* I glanced over and grabbed a magazine, breathing deeply. *I'm lying on the ground facing the ceiling, and Russell is playfully kicking me, telling me to get up.* I blinked my eyes a few times and took a deep breath.

"You all right, Brett?" my mom asked.

"Yeah, I'm fine."

As we waited, I fell into a deeper state of reflection. *Okay, so I grow up fine, working hard in school and having everything I needed. Okay, I didn't do anything wrong there. Did the best I could every day. I have an older brother who introduces me to weed, but I smoke less than most of my friends. I am the captain of the high school basketball team and starter on the eighteen and under Jewish national team. Okay, nothing weird about any of that. Just like anyone else. I go to college and party like anyone else. I was actually one of the lightweights in my group of friends! They did all sorts of drugs that were more intense than weed. Okay, so apparently the weed led to an insanely random group of isolated things that happened that weren't my fault. I end up in a psych ward, somehow? So weird. I do what I'm supposed to do and recover after almost two years of misery and get my life back. Okay, so that was behind me, and I had no clue it would ever happen again. They didn't tell me much. My life moves forward, and I get really good at online poker. I graduate college and make a shit ton of money, enough that I don't need to get a real job. My friends are all impressed. I get a little bored and start smoking again. That's on me, but no one told me not to! So I have another round of these insanely weird, random events and get my ass kicked by a bunch of cops. I survive the hospital experience and recover, just like I'm supposed to. They tell me not to smoke any more weed and this won't happen again. I follow their orders exactly and make a career for myself without even playing online poker! Weird mental stuff behind me, no more weed, and I'm working a good, clean job. So I move to a new city to help my brother out with his business, and we crush it! I'm managing a bunch of people and figuring out things as I go every day. Then I have another round of bullshit? Another round of hospitalization? And here I am, bipolar, recovering again, feeling like shit. There was no weed in the picture! None of this makes any sense. How could this have happened to me?*

A shorter woman with a friendly aura poked her head into the waiting room. "Brett?"

"Yep, that's me."

"Come on back. I'll see you now."

INSTANT EDUCATION

"Have a seat wherever you like," she said.

I scanned her office and observed an L-shaped couch in the corner with African-themed pillows. I was reminded of previous hallucinations that I had of tracing an L-shape on my kitchen counter back in Texas and believing that I was being evaluated by the TV alone in my apartment. Next to one end of the couch was a single seat with a white cushion that I could sink into that looked comfortable. *Okay, she might want me to*—I interrupted my analysis of the chair-selection routine and chose the white seat. I was too exhausted and over all this. I felt a sense that she already knew everything about me, which made this introduction even more awkward.

"Okay, Brett. Before we get started, I want you to take this depression survey."

She handed me a packet of multiple-choice questions and gave me some time to complete it before we moved on. I complied as usual and flipped open the packet of fifty questions or so. *Do any of these researchers understand that this is the most biased, unuseful tool that exists?* I started flying through the questions, checking off boxes after only reading a word or two of the questions. *I'm in deep shit if this is how she's learning about my current state.* I finally finished and handed it over to her with a smile, like I was happy and interested in the results.

Then she started a conversation in a manner that no other medical professional had in the last ten years of mania, hospitalizations, and depression that had owned my life.

"Brett," she said after tossing the depression survey on her desk. "You are a very interesting man from what I hear. Your mother loves you very much, and that is why she wanted us to work together. She explained to me that you are a good student, have been very successful, and will do what it takes to get better. I can already see those qualities in the short time that we have been together today. I'm sure you have told your story a lot, but would you mind sharing it with me? It will be very helpful."

Upon hearing these words, I felt emotional because what she was saying was true. It had been such a tough road, and she helped me remember who I was, and for the first time in a long time, there was no judgmental voice in my head.

I started from the beginning and described in as much as I could about growing up, family history, all three episodes, and more. I noticed that she paid very close attention to the concussion that I had during my senior year of high school basketball, something that others didn't focus on, aside from Dr. E. She took notes on every word that I said, which made me want to share more. After twenty minutes or so, she put her pen and pad down and sat back in her chair while sighing deeply. She appeared to be affected on a deeper level by my story.

She sat up and pulled herself together, which forced a reaction in me to do the same. "Brett"—she took a deep breath—"you've been through a lot. I can compare what you've been through to your brain being on fire."

I pictured a log cabin in the woods going up in flames while firefighters rushed to the scene with hoses and other equipment. *That serious, huh.*

"I also believe you can recover from this with daily maintenance." She hopped up and retrieved a small wooden box that had about fifteen small objects in it, ranging from a small hammer to a penny. We worked through an exercise that reinforced that my brain was functioning just fine even after being on fire.

She switched her demeanor from comforting to stern after the exercise. "Brett, omega-3 fish oils are a great mood stabilizer. Go to a pharmacy right after this and make sure you have enough of the

1000 mg or 300 mg pills to take three times per day starting now. It's over the counter."

Whoa, whoa, whoa, slow down. "Do I take it with food?"

"Yes," she said.

My heart started to race. "Okay, got it." *Three more pills per day, great.*

She handed me a card with the right bottle to get. "We are running out of time for today, Brett, but before you go, I'm going to teach you a breathing exercise called square breathing. It's essentially like taking an anxiety pill without having to take the medication."

More stuff? I felt a bit overwhelmed thinking about the fish oil still. I thought that if I messed this up, I would ruin everything.

"Breathe in for four seconds, hold for four seconds, breathe out for four seconds, don't breathe for four seconds. Repeat four times. Got it?"

"Uh, yeah, I guess."

"Let's practice one time."

Breathe in. One, two, three, four. Hold. One, two, three, four. Breathe out. One, two, three, four. Don't breathe. One, two, three, four. Oooh, I like this one. I felt at ease for a few seconds.

"Okay, do these three times per day. See you next session."

HOPELESS WANDERER

When I made eye contact with my mom after leaving Dr. F's office, I gave her a look that said, "We have work to do." It was much different from the look I gave her ten years ago leaving this office on the way to the psych ward that said, "I'm excited." And even more different from the look I gave her locked inside the unit while she left that said, "How could you leave me here?" My mind was moving fast now, aware that I needed to acquire the fish oil and be the best at square breathing.

"Mom," I said as we walked down the street to our car, "we have to go to a pharmacy and pick up fish oils now! I have to take these pills three times per day. Dr. F said so."

"Okay, Brett, let's go straight from here."

On the drive over, I was hyper while explaining to her what square breathing is. "Okay, so basically you have to breathe in for four seconds, hold for four seconds, breathe out for four seconds, and then stop breathing for four seconds. You repeat it four times and do it three times per day." She had an optimistic look on her face. "Do you want to try it with me right now?" I asked.

"Sure," she said. We spent the short drive to the pharmacy completing a square breathing exercise. *Okay, one square breathing exercise down. Three exercises per day, every day for the rest of my life. Let's say I live another fifty years, only 18,250 exercises to go!* The excitement slowed when we parked in the CVS parking lot.

"Do you want me to go in with you?" my mom asked.

I wish I could've answered no, but I answered yes because I was afraid of what might happen in there.

I took a step through the automatic sliding door and saw my mom out of the corner of my eye next to me. *Is it okay if I do more than three square breathing exercises per day?* I assumed that Dr. F would answer yes to this question. I'd been in this CVS many times before but never had to look in the vitamin section. I felt anxious and was reminded how crippled I still was by shots of anxiety hitting my stomach with every breath. *Breathe in. One, two, three, four.* The anxiety settled a bit. I decided that I would browse every aisle until I randomly came across my section because the store wasn't that big. I wandered toward the makeup section. *Why am I in the makeup section? Hold. One, two, three, four.* Two women in the aisle looked over at me and giggled. *Ugh, they can tell I have no clue where I am going.* I regained my focus and kept moving. *Breathe out. One, two, three, four.*

"Brett!" I heard my mom call from the correct aisles. "Brett, where are you?"

Ugh, how embarrassing. I followed my mom's voice to the correct aisle. *Don't breathe. One, two, three, four.* I noticed how one cycle of square breathing helped me navigate the nightmare of anxiety that had shown in the makeup aisle. I felt slightly better and didn't finish the other two cycles because I had already done the exercise twice today. One more later, and I'd have three under my belt.

I looked up and saw my mom scanning the aisle, and I decided to copy her. *Okay, here we go.* I lost my balance a bit and became light-headed. *What's that all about?* I heard my mom's voice nagging me to tell Dr. F about every little thing and took a mental note of this newfound wobble. I put my hand on the shelf to help balance and started reading the pill bottles. *Airborne, no. Magnesium, no. Vitamin gummies. Hmm, these look delicious, but no. Protein shakes. Okay, this is the wrong direction.* I glanced at my mom.

"Here it is." She was standing in front of the sea of fish oils on the counter. *Sea of fish oils, heh.* I took a deep breath and saw that there were different combinations of dosages and amounts. Finally, we both honed in on the correct bottle and felt relieved.

"Brett? How are you? It's been so long!"

Ah, shit. An old friend from high school caught me before I could leave the store. "Hey! I'm good. How are you?" *There is no chance in hell that she's buying this.*

"I'm good, Brett, thanks." Then she went on for the next five minutes about things that I didn't ask about. I did another round of square breathing while she was talking because why not? My mom was part of the conversation as well, and somehow, I left the store with her business card.

"Was that conversation hard for you?" she asked when we got back into the car.

She's finally getting it. "Yes, I'm sure she could tell something was wrong with me."

My mom replied with a warm smile, "I'm not so sure, Brett. I'm not so sure."

THE WHITEBOARD

After all the trying, all the listening, and all the vulnerability and stress, I still felt the same hell-like buzz while lying in bed the next morning. *Why do I still feel this way? This is my life now.* On hard mornings like this one, my mind would only focus on the negatives, completely separating from any progress that had been made over the last several months. I was scared thinking about the laundry list of things that I had to do just to get even. *Get up, square breathing, meds, breakfast, blah blah blah.* Today, everything felt hard. *What if I forget this? What if I take the wrong dose of that?*

I was lying on my back, staring at the white ceiling, when bold numbers and letters started forming and floating into my frame of vision. My automatic breathing kicked in, and some of the anxiety vanished. *Keep staring, keep staring.* Then the collage of numbers and letters started forming into small segments like *AM, PM, Sat, Tue, Wed, Mon, Th, Fri,* and *Sun. The days of the week! Keep staring, keep staring.* Short dashes floated their way in between some of the numbers which connected and read like 9-10, 8-9, 10-11, 11-12, 5-6, 12-1, 7-8, 1-2, 3-4, 4-5, 2-3, and 6-7. *Those have to be times of day. Keep staring, keep staring.* The days of the week arranged themselves across the top of the ceiling while the time ranges fell down the side in order with *AM* and *PM* in the appropriate slots for morning, afternoon, and evening. *Okay, this is some sort of schedule. Keep staring, keep staring.* There were still a pile of letters mixed together in the middle of the schedule, which started forming into words like *psychiatrist, breathing, lucky, meds, to, alive, psychologist, square, be, workout,* and others. The words floated into the appropriate spots, and the hell-like buzz was no more.

I took what physically felt like the same step out of bed onto the warm carpet that I had when I first came home, but psychologically, my step was determined and with purpose. I settled in for square breathing and made myself a few hard-boiled eggs for breakfast. I skipped the Ativan and took my meds two pills at a time, including the large fish oils that were recently added.

"Mom, I'm going to get a whiteboard!" I yelled up to my mom, who wasn't in the kitchen with me. Instead of flying out impulsively, I waited for her to acknowledge and approve my request. I breathed slowly as I entered Karen's car, appreciating that she lent it to me. *Come and get some.* I turned on the radio, ready to experience whatever was in store for my short drive to Walmart. A familiar song came on the radio, which I was able to listen to as a song and not anything else. *Breathe in, breathe out. When the radio says* he, *that isn't you.* I make it to the large parking lot and see an open spot toward the front. *There's no reason I can't drive up and take that spot.* I passed many easier spots that were farther away to take the convenient spot up front, something that I wouldn't have thought twice about before the bipolar mess.

I walked into Walmart and was punched with a hit of anxiety which threw me off-balance. I leaned up against the wall and took a deep breath. *You are so close. Push through this.* I started walking through a random aisle, repeating the same mistake that I had made at CVS while looking for the fish oils. I stopped myself and noticed an employee twiddling his thumbs. *Screw it, I can do this.* I walked directly to him. "Hi, sir, can you tell me where the whiteboards are?"

"Of course, follow me."

That wasn't so bad. He took me to the appropriate section, and I found what I needed. I was able to pay for it and make it home with no major issues.

I rushed the whiteboard up to my room and set it on my bed, facing up at the white ceiling. My mom popped her head in. "What a good idea, Brett."

"Thanks," I said, less bothered by her engagement. I took a few minutes to mirror the mental image I had of my schedule on the ceiling this morning and transfer it to the whiteboard. I had my few morning routine events, square breathing exercises, and med reminders written in the appropriate time slots. When I was finished and organized, I felt like I had something to work off, somewhere to go from here. *Okay, I'm going to put every new thing that I do on this whiteboard. If something is scheduled, I'm going to do it.*

I couldn't help but remember that the words *alive, to, lucky,* and *be* were part of my morning dream. I recalled driving 110 on the highway, being restrained by four cops, looking over a bridge and almost jumping, and yelling at a crowd full of people aggressively in a public pizza place; all things that I had done over the past decade as a result of my illness. I then made room for an additional spot at the start of every day. It read, "Lucky to be alive."

CHECK-INS

"How are you, Brett?" my younger brother, Russell, checked in as usual.

"I think I had a good day yesterday," I replied.

"Yeah? What happened?" he asked.

"Well, it's obviously not a huge deal or anything, and I'm still a loser with no future, but I went to the store and got a whiteboard from Walmart. I actually made a calendar for myself that I can use to stay organized with meds and stuff."

"That's awesome, dude! I'm proud of you," he said with excitement.

"How are you doing?" I felt it necessary to ask even though I didn't have the energy to care deeply about what was being said by him or anyone else about their own lives.

"I'm good. Hang in there, B."

It's like he can tell that I wasn't going to care about whatever he was going to say. "Will do."

I hung up the phone and decided to parlay this bump in confidence by calling my older brother, Jerry.

He answered, "Hey, man, what's up?"

"Nothing, just feel like I haven't talked to you in a while. What are you up to?"

"Oh, just still working hard at Systems Fit. Things aren't the same since you left, but we are managing. A few of the staff and our partners that you were working with asked how you are doing."

That's nice. "Ah, that's cool," I replied.

"Our office manager said that he could sense something was going on with you in those final days before the sickness got to you. He said you barged into his office and told him that everyone needed to be hydrated and have the best water in Texas available to them."

Ugh, that's kind of embarrassing. I laughed nervously. "Ha ha, wow, that's messed up. I think I remember doing that, actually."

"How are you doing?" he asked.

"I'm fine, just got all proud of myself for writing a lame schedule on a whiteboard. This fucking sucks."

"Honestly, Brett, we all need to do that. Nothing to feel bad about," he replied.

"Yeah, I guess."

"Well, hang in there and talk soon."

"Okay, bye."

Okay, that went pretty well. I looked at the whiteboard and saw how open my evenings were. I decided to call a friend and make plans like old times. "Roger! What are you up to tonight?"

"Nothing, man, probably just hangin' in and watching some B-ball. Welcome to stop by."

"Sounds good. I'll be over."

"Cool, see you then." I hung up the phone and instantly regretted that third phone call. *What if other people are there? What if I forget to do something? I mean, I guess I could look at it on my phone, but I also don't want to be on my phone the whole time.* Then I had an incoming call from my dad.

"Hey, Brett, how are you? How are you keeping busy?"

He was the one that I had to sound the most healthy for. "I'm doing really well. I actually drove myself to Walmart and got a whiteboard today. I'm using it to keep track of my schedule."

After a second or two of silence, he said, "Good." And that was about all that I got. "Well, I was just checking in. Glad you are doing well."

"Thank you, bye."

I spent the next couple of hours feeling anxious about going to Roger's. Somewhere in that time, Sierra texted me. *I'm so much more comfortable around her than my high school friends who drink. There won't be alcohol at her place.* I felt very guilty but made up an excuse to Roger that I couldn't come over so I could hang out with Sierra. In my mind, it was a huge deal, but he couldn't care less; that was the type of friendship that we had. When I arrived at Sierra's, it was a bit more comfortable than previous times. I told her about some of the things that were getting better but was sure to remind her of the traumatic things that had happened in my episodes and some of the hard things that I was still dealing with. We watched a few episodes of *Broad City*, and then I went home.

That night, I reflected more deeply on what my life was like now. Almost everything that I was doing in a day now would have been almost insignificant in my previous life. *Calling a couple friends? Going to the store by myself? Big whoop. I used to work my ass off and handle hard things with little effort.* But something was different now. I was starting to understand that something special could come from terribly hard experiences. The perspective that one gained from going through hardship could never have been achieved without that hardship. I had a sense that something special was happening inside me.

MEDITATION

Ohhhm. Ohhhm. I sat up straight in bed with my heels and fingers touching like a Buddha master. *Ohhhm.* I laughed to myself, thinking about how foolish I must look. I took a deep breath and started the free meditation app that I had downloaded.

"Welcome to this beginner's meditation exercise. I will guide you through every step of the way."

Well, that's nice, just do what he tells me to do, and I'll unlock a new part of myself.

"Find a place where you can be upright, with your feet flat on the floor and your hands resting on your lap."

I paused the app and moved to the computer chair in my room. *Ah, much better.*

"Start by taking three deep breaths in and out."

I took three deep breaths following the teacher's instructions. *Ah, that feels nice.*

"Now close your eyes and turn your attention to the breath, noticing the rising and falling of your chest. Say 'breathe in' to yourself on the in breaths and 'breathe out' to yourself on the out breaths. If you get distracted, gently bring your attention back to the breath."

I closed my eyes. *Breathe in. Breathe out. Breathe in. Breathe out. Did I run out of medication yet?* I saw an image of hundreds of pills falling from a cliff like a waterfall. *I should probably go check. I will go check.* I felt anxious and broke the meditation to go check downstairs. I saw that I had more than enough pills and went back upstairs to meditate again. I sat down. *Okay, breathing in, breathing out. Not doing this.* I quit and turned off the app. *That was so weak. You can't even sit still for ten minutes.* I was caught in a tough spot because the purpose of mediation was to let thoughts come and go, and there was no way to "meditate harder."

So I skipped the meditation and let it ruin the whole morning for me. I felt a strong urge to compensate for my failure and thought that organizing my pills in a better way might eliminate some of the uncertainty and worry that I experienced. My mom happened to have a pillbox that suited my needs. It had three rows and seven columns covering the three doses of medication that I'd have to take seven days per week. She also had a single-row pillbox that I could use for my early-morning meds. When I added the arsenal of pills, I couldn't believe how many I was taking in the course of one week. I dumped them all out and took a picture for my brothers to see. *#bipolarlife.* This image hit home, and they both showed sympathy.

Dr. F had been working closely with me to find the right cocktail of meds. The lithium was a must, and fish oil was an easy win. I went to her office for an appointment, and meds were the main topic.

"Brett, I'm going to start you on a drug called Lamictal. Lamictal is a mood stabilizer and will complement the lithium. I'd like to get you up to 200 mg per day, but we cannot start there because it will take time for your body to adjust. If we go too fast, you may develop a fatal skin condition."

Fatal skin condition? "Fatal skin condition?" I replied with concern.

"Yes, this is something I have to tell you, but you'll be fine if we start at a low dose, increase gradually, and you are compliant as usual."

"Okay," I replied.

"Mom, what the fuck!" I came home worried. "I have to take this new drug called Lamictal. If I screw it up, then I'm going to die of a skin disease!"

She showed concern as well. "Let's call Russell."

Russell was in his final years of school becoming a dermatopathologist. He reassured us that it would be fine, and it was just something Dr. F had to say before prescribing. I had to take one pill in the morning to start. I decided to take all my medicine upstairs to my bathroom so I could own the responsibility. *Mom won't be here forever.*

I was looking in the mirror with no shirt on and basketball shorts, looking down at pillboxes full of pills of different colors, shapes, and sizes. *Don't mess this up.* My hands trembled as I opened the one for tonight. *Wednesday, night.* I inspected each pill individually to ensure I was taking the right one. *If I mess this up, then I'm dead.* I downed all the pills at once and nearly choke. *They make that look so easy in the movies!* I moped back into my room and saw the whiteboard, organized but still pretty empty. *What am I doing with my life?* I took slow steps downstairs and saw the puzzle with major progress made. *But it's only a puzzle.* I turned on the TV.

He's—

He isn't me.

Gotta make sure to put more sugar in these cookies next time.

I took a deep breath and connected my early mediation with my ability to let the hallucination come and go.

I felt depressed that night. There were so many internal changes happening, but it didn't feel like real progress. I felt like a stuck adult living with my mom and working on a puzzle. No one could argue these tangible facts.

THE SECOND THOUGHT

"I'm just not myself. Bottom line," I said to Dr. E across from him while sitting on that familiar maroon couch. "Nothing is getting better! I used to manage large teams of people, take business trips across the country, and live independently in a beautiful city. Now I'm at home alone, with my mom. I can't do anything!" It was clear that some of my energy was back, however negatively it was coming out. I continued, "I have bipolar now, and there's nothing I can do about it. My life is different, forever. I'll never be the same."

He wrote and wrote and wrote then put his pencil and pad down and sat up, ready to untangle the mess of thoughts and phrases that I had just thrown up. "Listen to what you are doing," he said with a smile that showed how ridiculous I sounded. "Talk to me more about what you can't do."

He's onto me. "I can't leave the house comfortably, for one. Can't get a job, don't have any friends, can barely drive."

He gave the same look, then went in for the teachable moment. "Brett, how did you get here?"

I sat back and laughed nervously. "I drove." We shared a comical moment.

"So what makes you think that you can't drive?"

"Okay, I can drive. It just doesn't feel the same. Nothing feels the same."

"And why might that be?" he asked.

"Because I have bipolar."

"Well, maybe, have you seen any progress in the way you feel over the last few months?"

"No, everything still sucks."

Then he got real with me instead of explaining to me how far I've come, something that I needed. "Come on, Brett. Let me ask you this. What is your job?"

My job? "I have no job. I'm unemployed, as we both know," I replied.

"No, but what is your job right now? What do you have to do every day?" he asked.

"Take my medicine?"

"Good," he said.

"Show up to doctor's appointments?"

"Yep."

"That's all I can think of."

"Meditate? Work out? Try to socialize?" he asked.

"Yeah, I guess."

"And are you doing all those things?"

"Yes."

"Okay, then you are doing your job. When your thoughts are telling you otherwise, remind yourself to do your job."

"Yes, but that's the hard part. My thoughts are overpowering my ability to do that."

"Brett, I understand that. We are all wired differently, and you may just be someone whose initial thoughts are very powerful. That may even be part of the reason that you have been successful in your life. But I want you to think of it like this. Try to notice when the first powerful thought comes in."

Notice when the first powerful thought comes in.

"Understand that there is nothing you can do about that thought. That thought is hardwired in."

Understand that it's hardwired in.

"Then trust that the following thought or second thought is the one that you can control and own."

Control the second thought. "Okay, I got it."

I felt a sense of calm as I walked out of his office and to the elevator. I tapped my foot while waiting. *Where to now? Nothing to do, nowhere to be. Okay, that's the first thought. Nothing I can do about that one. I could actually go to the gym this afternoon. Okay, that's the second thought, the one that I can control.* It made sense to me.

But just because I could control the second thought and know the best move, it didn't mean I had the motivation to go and do it. *But what's my job?* I recalled that going to the gym was part of my job right now. Yes, it was not a paying job that I went to an office for, but it was my job right now as an individual with bipolar disorder, to invest in my health. This was the motivating factor. This was what got me to lace up my shoes and go to the gym.

But the gym was still a scary place with distracting hallucinations and the physical pain of working out. *But what is my job?* My job was to go to the gym and deal with it. *I'm not going to give up on myself. Today, I'm going to do my job. Today, I'm taking control of that bullshit hardwired thought that wants me to fail.* Nothing about the gym was comfortable that day, but when I pushed through and got home, it felt like I had put in a full day's work. I was fully engaged in therapy, did my mental homework, and applied it to the gym. I wasn't terribly proud of myself at the end of the day, but I was more aware of my flawed thinking and felt strong enough to do it all over again the next day.

Do Your Job

It was one step forward and two steps backward for the next few weeks. No matter what progress was made or how hard I tried to pump myself up, my mood was in full control of what I actually did. I could calmly fall asleep with great intentions of making the next day a positive one and then wake up feeling anxious and depressed. I could have a solid morning and afternoon and then not be able to fall asleep that night. I was at the mercy of my mind. The whiteboard was one of the only things that remained constant. If something was on there, then I had to do it. I needed more guidance and communicated this to Dr. F in our next session.

"Hey, Dr. F."

"Hello, Brett. How are you?"

"I'm good, except I'm struggling to keep my mood consistent. It feels like the swings are randomly coming and going."

"Hmm, can you tell me more?" She had her pen and pad in hand.

"Yeah, uh, I mean, I feel like I could go into the day with the best of intentions but feel depressed and not up for it when the time comes. I also might be really tired and looking forward to a good night's rest and then toss and turn in bed all night, which messes up my mood for the following day. It's confusing and random," I explained.

"Okay, Brett, well, your levels seem good on the meds. Are you still doing the square breathing exercises that we talked about?"

"I am. I'm finding them very helpful. I'm up to eight rounds of eight, three times per day."

"That's very good, Brett. And you are staying hydrated?"

"Yeah, trying to," I replied.

"Staying hydrated is critical. I also want to review what we talked about with time management," she said. I nodded and thought about the whiteboard. "You must be the master of your own time and schedule regardless of how you feel. For example, if you have a huge chunk of open time on your schedule, then you should either fill it with an activity or mark it as free time. You shouldn't be uncertain of what you are doing and when. I'm very happy with how you've organized your whiteboard, but it's time to add more healthy events to it. Let's talk about your full morning routine. You've made so much progress." We laid out a plan for my full morning routine for the rest of the appointment.

The next morning, my eyes opened, and I was feeling that familiar rush of anxiety. *Okay, it's there. No surprise. No big deal, really. Do the routine regardless.* I moved to the bathroom and popped the early-morning Synthroid. The clock read 7:00 a.m. *Done, okay, one hour to kill before I can eat or drink.* I walked back to my bedroom and took a minute to make the bed, something I never did before having an hour on my hands in the morning. I used to have places to go and people to see. I went back to the bathroom and brushed my teeth. *Probably not the most efficient order of events, but I can work on that. Make the bed first, take the Synthroid, then brush your teeth.* I turned on the shower and breathed deeply into the steam. I had a flashback to a moment during my latest episode of steaming up my whole bathroom and shattering my computer screen against the wall. *Ugh, that was scary.* I took a nice long shower and made it back to my room where the bed was made. *That's actually kind of nice, isn't it?* The clock read 7:15 a.m. *Forty-five more minutes.* I took a seat in my meditation chair and completed my first square breathing exercise of the day. It was 7:20 a.m. I chose a ten-minute meditation exercise. I closed my eyes. *This is stupid. It's so hard to sit still. Go do something else. Breathing in, breathing out. How long has it been? Is this even working? I can't tell. Breathing in, breathing out.* But I didn't quit because mediation was on the whiteboard, and my mood shouldn't dictate my actions, the whiteboard should. It was 7:30 a.m. *This feels like the right time to stretch.* I still had thirty minutes before I could eat or drink, so I decided to stretch out my shoulders, hamstrings, quads, neck, and lower back. It was 7:40 a.m. I went downstairs and boiled some water. This usually took about ten minutes. I chatted with my mom to kill the ten minutes and then placed three eggs into the water. I set the timer for fifteen minutes and messed with the puzzle during the downtime. Before I knew it, 8:05 a.m. showed on the microwave, and it was time for more meds and food. I drank decaf coffee with my eggs and downed my pills with a few gulps of water. I sat back in my chair and realized that it didn't matter what mood I was in this morning or what mood I would be in tomorrow morning. I took control of my time and completed an hour's worth of self-care tasks. *Bipolar didn't take this hour from me. This was my hour. This will be my hour every morning moving forward. This is my morning routine.*

VULNERABILITY

"Brett, we need to be ready to leave by 8:00 a.m. tomorrow morning," my mom said as we chatted in the kitchen over dinner.

Sure, like you'll be ready to leave by then. "Okay." My mom and I had decided to take a trip to visit family in Chicago for a long weekend. Russell lived there with his wife in one part of the city, and my aunt and uncle lived close by. There was a ticket available for me to see *Hamilton*, but I didn't feel comfortable enough to go to the theater and be around that many people. *Ugh, I wanted to see that show.*

When my alarm went off the following morning, I was out of sorts. I didn't realize that my morning routine would feel different with the thought of the trip happening shortly after. I had left myself enough time but couldn't fall into the mediation and skipped stretches all together. As expected, I was ready and waiting for my mom before the long drive as the clock approached 8:30 a.m. *Go use the downtime to catch up on meditation and stretching. No, I already missed my chance, and the order is all screwed up. I can't do it.* These new thoughts of doubt were unexpected because I had been doing so well for the previous few weeks with the routine.

"Okay, I'm ready," she said.

"It's about time!" I replied, more irritated with my inability to do my morning routine than her being late for the trip.

I manned the wheel for the seven-hour drive. "Brett, are you sure you are able to drive the whole way? I'm happy to take a turn."

"Please stop asking me that," I answered harshly. *I'm not going to let bipolar stop me!* Once I had a taste of recovery, there was no turning back. Everything became linear, and I would not accept a setback.

91

When we finally arrived, I felt anxious and vulnerable. Not only was I seeing family that wasn't fully up to speed on my recovery, but hallucinations were settling back in after the long trip. We pulled up to my aunt's downtown apartment, and she came outside to greet us.

"The Stevens from another state! How are you?" She gave me a warm hug.

She can tell I'm not feeling well. She can tell I missed my morning routine! "I'm good." I smiled, hiding the inner pain.

For the rest of the trip, I tried to find comfortable places to sit where I wouldn't have to move. As every second passed, I became more anxious, wondering if others could tell that I was not myself. *Okay, look comfortable, answer questions if asked, take a deep breath.* Everyone told me that I looked great, which I had a hard time believing. We made the long trip home, and for the next few days, I couldn't understand why I felt so terrible. I brought these concerns to Dr. E.

"I had it going, and I was feeling very well. Then the smallest change in my routine threw me off. It's like I had to start all over again. I lost confidence and became paranoid."

"Well, you'll certainly want to tell Dr. F about all of this as well. It could be the medication. But it seems reasonable that pushing yourself to drive and placing yourself in that situation could cause a change in mood," he explained.

"But it felt like I lost all control."

"I can see that, but whose decision was it to drive the whole way without taking a break?"

"Mine."

"Yes, Brett, it's just something to be aware of. This may be one area that you need to pay closer attention to for now. If you were in a wheelchair and just getting back on your feet, would you sprint right away?"

"No," I replied.

"You've come a very long way already, but you are still just getting out of the chair and need to pace yourself."

"Okay, makes sense."

"It's also important to understand that recovery isn't linear. You will make strides but also have setbacks. The key is to not give up on yourself and see that you are improving overall," he said.

"But it doesn't feel like it. The main takeaway from the trip that I got was that I'm too weak to take a short weekend trip. It makes me not want to try anymore," I replied.

"I can see why you feel that way," he said, "but that fact that you went on the trip in the first place is major progress!"

"Yeah, I guess."

On the drive home, I observed my thoughts. *I pretty much just told him what he wanted to hear for an hour. I don't think any of this is working. I can't do this.* I felt anxious about the scheduled workout I had that afternoon and skipped it. I sat with my anxiety for the rest of the day and couldn't sleep that night, comparing myself to my brothers and peers and discounting any progress that had been made. I erased the whiteboard in frustration.

TIME MANAGEMENT

The only thing on my schedule the next day was an appointment with Dr. F in the afternoon. The first thing I saw when I opened my eyes was the blank whiteboard. *Why did I do that? So dramatic.* But the anxiety was still there. I justified skipping meditation and stretching again because I could spill my heart out to Dr. F in the afternoon and then hopefully pick it back up tomorrow. The rest of the morning was spent on the puzzle and feeling bad for myself. *Tried to take a little trip? That's way too much for me. Back to your new life of dependence and puzzles.*

"All right, Brett, catch me up!" Dr. F had energy today and was ready to get to work. "How was the trip?"

Give it to her straight. "Not good. It threw me off my routine and made me feel worse than before I went," I replied.

The smile on her face straightened out a bit. "Why did it do that?" she asked.

"I don't really know. I was thinking about the trip, so I skipped my routine. I tried to be normal again by driving the whole way, and I think it had a negative effect on me. Old symptoms were showing."

She asked a few more medical questions and thought a slight med adjustment might be in order, but our conversation was more directed toward why I skipped my routine. "Brett, remember to do your job, as Dr. E said."

"I know. I just couldn't do it. It seemed too hard." I felt embarrassed about erasing the whiteboard, so I kept that to myself.

"Brett, think about your whiteboard and consider this. Imagine that each activity and time slot is not stuck in one place. Yes, you need to take your medication at certain times of the day, and that should remain fixed, but the other events are flexible and can be moved. Does that make sense?"

Okay, so move the event squares around the whiteboard however I want, but just make sure I do them. "It does."

"And Brett, I know that we haven't added many new activities to the calendar, but have you thought about playing basketball or something?"

Hell no. "Nah, that's not really for me anymore." *There would be way too many expectations if I did that.*

"All right. Well, maybe research some volunteer work. I think more activity will move us in the right direction."

Not going to do that. "Okay, I'll look into it."

Then she went into her pile of notes that she had taken on every session and pulled out what she called The Matrix. When she first introduced the topic, I was zoning in and out, but I peeked down on the paper and saw four quadrants with different qualities and values of my own listed like family, success, honestly, and more. She reminded me that I was very goal-oriented and motivated by reward. This made me feel special, but I was having a hard time seeing those qualities in myself. We also talked about diet. As Dr. F went on about avocado and lean meats, I went on a memory trip.

The five of us are sitting around the dining room table with a huge bowl of salad, pounds of brisket, and a mountain of pasta. Jerry and I start crushing the salad while Russell picks at his. "Russell is skinny and weak!" Jerry looked at me, and we both gave Russell shit for not eating as much as we were. When it was time for the meat, however, we all went to town. We all ate until we couldn't move and were fully satisfied. Then dessert came. I blinked a few times.

"So we really need to stay away from carbs and be aware of portion sizes. Got it, Brett?"

"Yep, got it!"

I still wasn't going to the grocery store, but I told my mom to look for more of the foods that Dr. F prescribed. I found myself sending her labels and asking questions, to which she would respond instantly. I had always been aware of my big appetite and what foods were healthy, but I didn't realize how losing sight of my diet could throw me into a depressed mood. But it felt like just another thing I had to think and worry about that I didn't pay any mind to in my past life. I was gathering information but not motivated to use it and aware that my good moods would probably only be temporary before I started backsliding. It was hard to see the progress that everyone was so happy to tell me that I was making. It was the moments that I was alone and reflecting that were the most real to me. No one else was seeing that.

SUPPORT GROUPS

A light bulb went off. *Support groups!* I had been spinning my wheels on what to do to get out of the house and couldn't come up with anything until the thought of support groups came to me. Dr. F must have offered up the idea at some point, but I pushed it away. After months of working on my basic routine, I now saw the value in getting out of the house and meeting new people that I might be able to relate to.

It was morning, and I was ready to get into my car and find the nearest group. But first, I had to find one. I opened my laptop. *Groups. Google groups, no. Support Groups. Peer Support, Our Clubhouse, NAMI. Wow, how many of these things are there? Are there really this many people in need?* I researched for a half hour or so and soon realized that even with all these groups, the earliest I would be able to attend would be tomorrow night. I was upset because I knew that my mood might be different at that time.

And I was right. When the time came to make the hour drive to the group, I avoided it. And after I avoided it, I felt guilty. And after I felt guilty, I ate. So instead of attending a new event and moving forward, I was on the couch, eating pizza and moving backward. *It all happened so fast.* At that moment, I told myself that I would attend the next group no matter how I felt. I told my mom, too, for some accountability.

"You don't have to put that much pressure on yourself, Brett. See how you feel."

Like she would have any clue how to handle all of this. "No, I'm doing it, Mom!" I slammed my feet upstairs and wrote it on the whiteboard with red marker.

I stressed about attending the group the next day but pulled myself together and went on a new adventure.

"I'm so proud of you, Brett," my mom said.

"Be proud when I make it back without quitting," I replied. There was one huge spot in front of the library where the group would take place, and I passed it up. *No chance in hell I'm parallel parking.* I ended up parking ten minutes away and barely made it to the group on time. I took a deep breath, which helped with some of my panic and light-headedness, and found my seat at the rectangular table where about ten others were already seated. I glanced around the table and saw two women with tattoos, a middle-aged man with a sweater, and a few others that looked like they had their stuff together.

The leader of the group introduced me first because I was a new attendee. All the others seemed to know a lot about each other. I told my story briefly and without anxiety, which was unexpected. Their faces remained focused as I talked about near-death experiences during my episodes and traumatic hospitalizations. I was pleased to be finished sharing and noticed that they were very supportive and were not fazed by my stories. *These people understand.* I had a small sense of hope as it was my turn to listen to them.

One of the women shared next. "Hey all, I'm having a good week, actually. I've been fighting with my doctor about giving me more medication, and she's not hearing me." I couldn't help but judge. *Just do what she says then.* "And I've been doing better with socializing. My friend and I went to a concert last week and got hammered. It was a blast." *You have to be kidding me.* "But for some reason, the next day, I wasn't feeling well. I'm gonna have to go back to my doctor and figure it out. She really doesn't get me." *Hmm, maybe that could be from the "getting hammered" part?* The group was very proud of her, and a few others passed on sharing until it was the middle-aged man's turn.

"I'm not doing so well, guys. No matter what I do, I can't get my kids to call me." *Ah, that's tough.* "They just won't come around."

The leader of the group chimed in, "Do you think that might have something to do with the gambling?" he asked.

Oh boy. "Absolutely not. They both need to understand that gambling is something that is very important to me and be okay with it. It's really sad that they don't understand."

Yeah, that one is on you, buddy. He finished and the group ended.

On my drive home, I knew I would never go back to the group. While I did enjoy that everyone could relate to my stories, I didn't like the pity party and lack of accountability that I heard in their stories. I also felt good about going in the first place. It was not easy for me to drive there, stay for the whole time, and drive home. I still felt off and frustrated, but I was certain that I wouldn't use bipolar disorder as an excuse in my life. I found reassurance in the idea that my core values were still intact.

THE POKER PROJECT

Playing cards were spewed across the floor because the unfinished puzzle took up most of the table in the dining room. I was on the floor with my laptop next to me, typing furiously.

"What are you doing, Brett?" my mom asked.

"I'm putting everything I know about poker into an organized learning platform. I'm going to teach people in sequence from knowing nothing about the game, all the way through what the pros do. They'll learn everything I know and should be able to make big money like I was. You might be a good candidate." I smiled, feeling good about my latest addition to my schedule, The Poker Project. She didn't doubt my ability to take a person with no poker knowledge and turn them into a pro, making thousands of dollars, but she was concerned for another reason.

"Just make sure to pace yourself," she said.

"I know, I know." *I get it. I'm living with bipolar now and always have to watch everything I do.*

She had good reason to check on me. About eight years ago, I was playing poker professionally as my full-time job, about eighty hours a week, before having a public episode and involuntary admission to the local psych ward. I was walking on cars and resisting the police. She had seen me become engulfed in the game and wanted to make sure writing about poker wouldn't overtake my world and become my new obsession. I assured her that I would chart out time on my calendar and only work on the project during those hours. *So this life balance thing is kind of the opposite of how things used to be. Before, I was praised and told to move faster and work harder and longer.*

Now, I need to choose the amount of time I want to do something before I start and schedule it. It was a struggle for me, but during this first writing session, I noticed that my focus was extremely precise, and I was as productive as ever. I started with the basics and made a mental roadmap of each lesson. *Okay, okay, okay.* I felt a bit anxious. *What's the first thing someone would need to know? The cards! Don't assume that anyone understands that a king is greater than a queen. Start by writing a lesson about what beats what.*

Surprisingly, the mental energy used to write about poker made me more interested in going to the gym. It seemed to dull down some of the worries and hallucinations that I was still experiencing in public places. This activity closed a gap of restlessness because it was long enough and strenuous enough to make me feel productive, even though I was still alone and at home. I felt pride looking at my schedule. *Morning routine, breakfast, meds, The Poker Project, lunch, meds, workout.* It wasn't a full day, but it was a major improvement from the emptiness that had lived inside me for so long.

But as my mom cautioned, I became so obsessed with the work that I was unable to keep it inside the two-hour window. Not only would I spill out of the time slot, but I would then think about what I was going to write for the rest of the day. With the stress came anxiety and ultimately, sadness. I lost all motivation to continue working on The Poker Project after about a week of starting. One day, my old friend John called to check in.

"How we doin', B?"

"Eh, I'm all right. I'm trying to write out this poker thing that we used to talk about. It's too hard."

John had never known me to be a quitter and offered up an idea. "Why don't you just write about one hand at a time? Send the hand to me, and I'll edit it for you; then we can decide what we want to do with it. Maybe we can post it online as a blog or something."

"That actually sounds really good to me, thanks."

"No problem. I want to help you out in any way that I can." John was one of my best friends. He'd been there during my first episode in college and was also living in Texas when I experienced my most recent episode.

When we got off the call, I updated the whiteboard with only one time slot per week to work on a hand for The Poker Project. I also started using the calendar on my phone more seriously for events so I could set reminders, mainly for medications. When the time came for me to write the first article, I was pleasantly surprised at how easily the information poured out. It took me about thirty minutes to write about a full hand. John asked me to write four full articles before going live with the blog so that we had enough content for our potential subscribers.

I mentioned to Russell, Jerry, and my dad on separate phone calls that I was writing poker articles. They all responded sarcastically in their own loving ways but had a similar question for me, "Didn't you fail English in college?"

GOING PUBLIC

"I'm not doing it. I'm not making it public," I said to my mom in our usual hangout spot in the kitchen.

"But you've been saying all week that you think it's good and that people might actually like it," she replied.

"Well, I was wrong. It was a dumb idea in the first place," I continued.

"Well, let it settle in a bit. See how you feel tomorrow." My mom seemed fairly certain that I would want to release my poker blog when this mood passed.

I was frustrated with this unexpected anxiety and had an open day, so I decided to take a jog to blow off some steam. I took my phone and headphones with me to drown out my thoughts. I put on a song that would pump me up and turned it up loud as I started with a fast pace. A few seconds in, I decided to turn my light jog into an all-out sprint. My muscles hurt, and I was becoming out of breath. *Just go, just go, just go.* I needed to prove to myself that I was in control of something. *Just go, just go, just go.* I ran out of breath and gave up, slowing to a walk and taking my headphones off. *You have nothing. No control over your moods and no control of your physical body. Welcome to your new life. Okay, that's the first thought, the wired-in thought. Let that pass and pay attention to the second thought.* The second thought came in the same as the first. *You have nothing. No control over your moods and no control of your physical body. Welcome to your new life.* Well, it must be true. I had no ability to see the progress that I had made with my morning routine, new things like the support group, and The Poker Project. Everything was the same as before, and my thoughts reminded me of that.

As I continued to walk, I kept my focus on a large pine tree that jutted out onto the road. I kept breathing and saw it transform into a *Tyrannosaurus rex*. *I'm not afraid.* I walked straight up to the tree and ripped a few branches on my way back. I was in a very awkward place, still hallucinating but now with good awareness that it wasn't real. The depression and anxiety were more unfamiliar to me now than the mania. I laughed at myself for getting into a fight with a pine tree and headed back home. *This is seriously all one big joke. What the fuck am I afraid of? I have nothing more to lose. That blog is going out.*

"I am doing it. I am making the blog public."

My mom smiled and reassured me that it was going to be great. "I don't know how you wrote all that. I could never do it."

"Yeah, we'll see if anyone gives a shit."

I called John and told him to post the first four articles of The Poker Project blog. He was excited and helped me understand how to use social media to promote it. I had some background in marketing from my previous jobs and believed that if I shared the link to the blog with everyone in my phone that I would be able to develop a decent following right out of the gate.

In my previous jobs when I sold paper door-to-door, gym memberships, and gym software, I had no shame in calling on leads until they told me to stop or they bought what I was selling. I took a similar approach in promoting The Poker Project. I scrolled through the names in my phone and copied the link with a short message hundreds of times, without paying close attention to whom I was texting. I felt a buzz as the messages went out. What I didn't plan for was the types of responses I would get. Instead of subscriptions, I got replies like "Who is this?" "Brett! Long time no talk. How are you?" "What is this?" "What are you up to now?" "Where are you living now?" "Wanna meet up this weekend?" and so on. *Uh-oh.* I had just given myself a truckload of anxiety to deal with.

In our next session, Dr. F helped me come up with scripted responses to some of the replies like "This is Brett!" "I'm good," "It's a new project I'm working on," "I'm transitioning and looking into new careers," "In PA," and "I will let you know about this weekend." I worked through the messages one by one, which served as a way to practice my language on a nonthreatening platform. When the dust settled, a decent chunk of my contacts did subscribe to the blog. I felt a slight amount of pressure that I'd have to deliver for my audience every week, but that wasn't bipolar; that was normal. Anyone might feel that type of pressure in a situation like this. I recognized that this type of anxiety was different from the torture that I was used to. This was normal anxiety.

THE LIBRARY

I had been in a boxing ring for months and only able to take small jabs at bipolar, but understanding and applying the concept of normal anxiety served as my first uppercut in a winning round. *What else have I been beating myself up over that is just normal anxiety?* I thought about how anxious I would get in high school before having to give a presentation in front of the whole class. *That was normal.* I thought about my feelings before taking the SAT exam. *That was normal.* It was an important learning moment that shifted my perspective on what was related to the trauma of living with bipolar versus normal anxiety that I have always had.

One morning, I sat down to write my article of the week and my scope widened. *Let's do this somewhere else, treat it like work.* I thought about places close by in the community that would be quiet and nonthreatening. *The mall? Nowhere to sit. Starbucks? Too crowded and loud. The library? Perfect.* The library was a short drive away and across from my old middle school. I knocked out my afternoon square breathing exercise on the drive over, which settled me for a few seconds.

As I parked, I was flooded with negative thoughts about how lame it was that I was still so close to home. *I was so cool back in middle school, walking through this parking lot with my head held high. If I only knew then I'd be back here twenty years later.* I recognized that no matter how high my spirits were about learning some new things about myself, there was still a strong possibility that other thoughts could enter and ruin it. I tried the first thought, second thought tool, but it didn't work.

I finally had the courage to get out of my car and walk into the library with my laptop in hand. *Okay, yeah. I get the whole normal anxiety thing, but this is way more intense.* I took a deep breath and saw an empty table in the back corner. *Perfect.*

"Brett! How's your family doing?"

Shit. "Oh hey, Mr. C. Everyone is great." I kept moving as Mr. C, an old family friend, followed. *Shit.*

"So what are you up to now?"

I felt anxious and off-balance. *Is this normal?* "Oh, I'm just working on a project." I raised the laptop, indicating that I was here to work.

"Very nice. Where are you living these days?"

Shit. "Well, I'm just living with my mom." *Lame.*

"Oh okay, well, tell everyone I said hi."

"Okay, will do." He walked away, and I made a beeline to the empty table. *Ah, finally.* The calm voices and quiet noises of the library were soothing, and I was able to work on my article in peace. I enjoyed working here much better than at home. I decided that this would be my new office. *As painful as it was to run into Mr. C, I handled it.*

I noticed a small diner up the road and decided that I would eat there once my article was done. Then my phone buzzed, and the message read, "Meds."

Shit, I forgot to bring my meds. I started to panic a bit and packed my things up quickly. *Shit, shit, shit.* It had been so easy to be regimented when I wasn't going far away from my house, but I extended my range, and it had made me less aware. I made it home safely and had lunch, followed by the meds. I didn't beat myself up for forgetting them because I was in good spirits about the library, but I did worry about what would happen if I missed a dose. *Will I have another episode?*

When the time came to write my next article, I was ready. *Wake up, make bed, Synthroid, brush teeth, shower, square breathing, meditate, stretch, breakfast, meds, pack afternoon meds, library, square breathing, article, lunch, afternoon meds.* I had knocked out a seriously productive half day and was so focused on my activities that overcoming both normal and traumatic anxiety was doable. When I closed my laptop, I took a second to look out of the window and appreciated the sunlight. *This isn't so bad.* I finally gave myself a second to stop worrying and enjoy the moment. On my way out of the library, I ran into Mr. C again, and we chatted it up for a few more minutes. I felt more comfortable and let him in on more about The Poker Project. I wanted to tell him all about bipolar, but something didn't feel right. I had already had discussions with Dr. F about public versus private thoughts and sorting out the difference. *There's no reason for me to get into all that with him.*

We said our goodbyes, and on my way out, I noticed a shelf that held pamphlets for upcoming events going on at the library. I had a brief flashback to myself ripping down student event flyers on a bulletin board during my second public manic episode before being taken to the hospital by four police officers while I resisted. *Scary.* But I didn't make a manic scene in the library today. Today, I took a flyer out and read it through. "Adult Chess League. Every other Friday, 1–3." I thought about the whiteboard and my phone, already knowing that I had this time slot open. I folded up the flyer, tucked it into my pocket, and headed back to home base.

CHESS

I had been less anxious running out in front of thousands of fans for my high school basketball championship game than I was walking into a quiet room at the library with seven senior citizens playing chess. I stood quietly for a few minutes before anyone even noticed I was there.

"Can I help you?" asked one of the men after taking a few seconds to make out that there was a human being standing in the doorway.

Oh, you've got to be kidding me. "Yeah, uh, I'm here to play chess, I think?"

"Oh good. Guys, we have a new player!" he said with excitement. Then three of them looked up at me, and the other three slowly turned in their chairs to see who the new competition was.

"What's your name?" he asked.

"Brett," I replied.

"Hi, Brett," they all said at once like we were at an AA meeting and I had just introduced myself. *I'm Brett, and I play chess. Hi, Brett!*

"You can have a seat over here and play against Arthur."

I walked over empty handed and started setting up the pieces on his board.

"You can play white," he said. White has a slight advantage over black because white moves first.

Wow, this guy is giving me a head start. I thought about how I had beaten a top-level executive on a business trip at my last job, gaining respect from him and his company. *I think I can handle this old guy.* I noticed that I still had some of my ego and competitive fire inside me even while on medication and battling bipolar disorder. I took a moment to realize that none of these men had any idea that I live with the condition. *If they only knew what I was going through, then they'd be impressed that I'm here.* I'd been through enough therapy to know that that thought was really directed toward my dad, not this group of old men that I had just met.

So I came out with my usual opening, not terribly focused and assuming I would win. A few moves later, the game shifted, and it was very clear that I was the inferior player. One of the other men sitting next to us glanced at our board and laughed. "He's rated 1900, Brett."

Oh wow. Arthur whooped me and didn't want to play again because I wasn't near his level, which was proper etiquette for chess. I was interested in my own reaction to losing. Usually, I would be hard on myself and needed to play another game until I could win. But today, in this quiet room with these peaceful old men, I did not feel the competitive rage that I had become so accustomed to over the years. I was okay with losing.

I rotated around and got to meet the full group of guys. I answered questions about where I was from and what I did, in a similar tone that I had with Mr. C. I recognized that this was a public, nonthreatening place to practice my social skills, having little on the line. I enjoyed listening to their stories and appreciated how skilled they were at a game that I loved so much. I could learn from them.

At the end of the session, one of the gentlemen let me know that there was a formal team that he coached that played competitively at the downtown university once a month. He asked if I'd be on the team, and I told him I would think about it. *Now that would be a big deal.* I was also aware that I'd be in the same place where I had my second episode and near the same psychiatric hospital where I was involuntarily committed.

I took the opportunity after chess to take inventory of my current situation. *Okay, I have bipolar disorder. I get it. I have a morning routine that is clearly helping, and I will do everything I can to never miss meds and breathing exercises. I will continue to work out and be aware of my diet. I will work on The Poker Project and continue to show up for chess. I will report anything weird that happens to my doctors. This is my job right now.*

My dad checked in that night. "Hey, Brett, what's up?"

"Oh, nothing. I'm still working on The Poker Project, and I actually played some chess today."

"Good," he replied. "You making any money doing that?"

I answered, "No, but The Poker Project actually has some potential. Chess is just for something to do."

"Are you still working out?" he asked.

"Yes."

"Good," he said. "Well, hang in there."

"Will do," I replied. I spent the rest of the night feeling anxious about what my future career would be, feeling like the progress that I had made was insignificant.

EATING ALONE

Breathe in for eight seconds. One one thousand, two one thousand, three one thousand, four one thousand, five one thousand, six one thousand, seven one thousand, eight one thousand. Hold it for eight seconds. One one thousand, two one thousand, three one thousand, four one thousand, five one thousand, six one thousand, seven one thousand, eight one thousand. Breathe out for eight seconds. One one thousand, two one thousand, three one thousand, four one thousand, five one thousand, six one thousand, seven one thousand, eight one thousand. Don't breathe for eight seconds. One one thousand, two one thousand, three one thousand, four one thousand, five one thousand, six one thousand, seven one thousand, eight one thousand. Seven more to go.

I skipped my square breathing exercise as part of my morning routine today and was making it up on the car ride to breakfast. On some mornings, I'd practice intentionally switching around the order of things to make my brain more malleable. Today, I decided that I'd head to the local diner for breakfast and use the short drive as time to do my breathing exercise. I was sure to do the other parts of my routine like meditating and meds before I left. I parked the car and took one last deep breath, aware that this self-induced social test to get breakfast by myself wouldn't be easy.

"How many in your party?" the greeter asked.

"Oh, just one."

"Right this way." I followed her through the crowded restaurant and heard hints of hallucinations.

That's him. Should he be here alone? What a loser.

I took a deep breath and reminded myself to just let it pass. She showed me a four-person booth, and I had a seat. Then new, similar hallucinations occurred, but I used the same tactic of letting other's voices referencing me pass. *This wasn't as intense as at the library.* I moved my attention to the menu that was already at the table and read it top to bottom, another test of my ability to read and focus and something I would not have been able to do months ago.

"Hey there!" A friendly waitress appeared and asked me what I'd like to drink.

"Coffee, please. Oh, and make it decaf!" I imagined her face judging a person of my age drinking decaf in the morning. *It's because I have bipolar.*

"Coming right up!" she said. I chose an egg white omelet and twiddled my thumbs until she came back with the joe.

"This is decaf?" I asked. My aunt, who also didn't drink caffeine, taught me to confirm with the server just to be sure.

"Oh, uh, I'm so sorry. This is regular. Let me go back and get you another."

"Okay, no problem. You can also put in an egg white omelet for my meal." She nodded, and I tucked the menu back where it originated. *Good thing I checked.*

The hallucinations subsided, and I had a few moments, out in public, feeling somewhat normal. Instead of acknowledging the progress that I had made, I instantly thought about how I was going to make money. *Are you making any money doing that?* My dad's voice echoed in my head. The waitress came back with my food and coffee, and I trusted that it was decaf.

"Here you go, and if you need creamer, it's over there."

I glanced over at the bowl of creamer single packets, took out two, and tore them open before adding them to my coffee. I couldn't find a spoon as the creamer floated in my drink, so I had to use the underside of the packet to stir my coffee. *Gross.*

Then it hit me. *I need to find a way for the packet to be the stirrer and the stirrer to be the packet!* My brothers and I had a group text going where we would float new business ideas out there for the other two of us to critique. I sent "a coffee creamer packet that will also serve as a stirrer." Both of them were confused, so I had to spell it out. "Have you ever not had a spoon around when trying to stir your coffee creamer in?" Jerry said that he had never had that problem in his life, but Russell thought it was brilliant. We made a pact to research the idea and have a weekly meeting to give updates and figure out what the next move should be.

"So maybe it could be a straw with both ends sealed and then you tear off one end, flip it, and then pour the creamer out on the other end?" Russell had thought more about the engineering behind our great invention.

"Yeah, that could work," I said.

"And I thought about the name, too, not that it's important at this point. But what do you think about Stir Eazy?" he asked.

"I love it," I replied. I purchased a thirty-dollar plastic sealer and sent it to him in Chicago. He stole a few straws from Starbucks for testing. We both knew this was all for fun, but it had a small chance of going somewhere. What was more valuable for me, however, was having a fun hour with my brother. Stir Eazy became my favorite scheduled event of the week.

AVOIDANCE

A healthy morning routine. *So what?* A few workouts. *Big deal.* A couple of hobbies and projects to kill some time. *Meaningless.* I was focused on the big picture today, and it still looked very scary. *Didn't you want to have a family one day? I'm pretty sure that will require you to leave your mom's house.* I couldn't shake the anxiety associated with becoming an independent person. My biggest fears came when thinking about socializing and being in front of others. I was so unsure of myself but sure that others would see the insecurity within me. I fantasized about the old days, which were still less than a year ago, where I was supremely confident and could own a room.

I was lucky to have resources like Dr. F and Dr. E available to help me work out these hard issues. I never took this for granted and spent time preparing for our meetings, realizing that the more I put into them, the more I would get out. Underneath the larger worries lay a small hope that things could indeed get better if I stuck with it. I brought my most recent issues to Dr. F.

"All right, Dr. F, riddle me this," I said comfortably in her office. We had built a nice rapport, and I could be myself in front of her. "I'm really struggling with this idea of being in social environments on a consistent basis. You saw how I've tried a few things but have quit when they became uncomfortable. I'm just not seeing the value or ability to overcome the thoughts that tell me that it's not worth doing."

She sat up in her chair after writing out every word I had just said. "Brett, do you know what avoidance is?" she asked.

"Uh, I think so. Isn't that when you just don't go to something?" I answered.

"Yes, it seems pretty obvious, but it's important that we take a second to discuss it." She put her pen down. "When we talk about avoidance, we aren't talking about your ability to work at something every day to become great at it. We are talking more about the things that you avoid because you aren't the best at it. Do you see what I'm saying?" she asked.

"Would it be the idea that I don't ever play softball because I'm not good at it?" I asked.

"Yes," she said. "It's hard for you to lighten up and just have fun playing softball without it becoming a competition and something that you need to perform in." *Yeah, I guess she's right.*

"Right now, you are avoiding these scary social situations because you are not at your best. You feel worried that it will be unpleasant, so you skip the event all together instead of just going and doing the best that you can. What are your thoughts on this interpretation?" she asked.

"Well, yeah. I definitely would like to feel comfortable when I go out. I mean, I've tried putting myself out there and had a panic attack. That was scary," I answered.

"Yes, I know, Brett. I'm not saying that you aren't trying, but it's important that you have this awareness so when you are confronted with another opportunity to get out there, you might see it differently."

I took a deep breath and felt a combination of anxiety and comfort. Anxiety because I knew I'd have to get out there more, and comfort because it was a step in the right direction.

"And also remember that the more you face the situation and do not avoid it, the easier and more normal it will become."

I left her office with something to think about. *Chess is a great thing. It forces me to be around people, and it's recurring. Working out is great also. Even though I'm working out alone, I'm in a room full of people. My other activities, like the morning routine, the puzzle, and The Poker Project, are all healthy hobbies that take up time, but they have me alone and at home.* I sat in my room when I got back, with a Sharpie in hand, ready to strategize. I recalled Dr. F telling me that volunteer work was a great way to gain back social skills while also helping a good cause. I wasn't thrilled about the idea, but I liked that I could quit or avoid the situation anytime that I wanted to. A real job with pay would not afford me that flexibility.

I was isolated and alone in Texas for much of the time that I was there, which led me to volunteer at a food bank on the weekends. That was a much different situation because I was the social one, proactively looking to meet new people and comfortable being outgoing. Now I was researching a volunteer opportunity that Dr. F recommended just to be around others and see if I could perform basic tasks. I was anxious as I filled out the online form for the opportunity that was a short drive away from my mom's house. The organization that I found helped organize excess medical equipment and sent them off to third world countries in need. This was a part-time opportunity, and it seemed to be a good fit. It felt like I was choosing the better of two terrible options when I submitted the form. *Do nothing and never become independent again, letting bipolar disorder run your life, or volunteer.*

VOLUNTEERING

I had to use every tool in the shed to show up for volunteering on day 1. I woke up somewhere in the gray area between normal anxiety and the hell-like buzz. *Is this feeling normal? Normal or not, I don't like it.* The whiteboard had a few activities on it before the afternoon volunteer event, so I used every ounce of my energy to redirect my focus toward doing what I was supposed to do. Dr. E's "Do your job" replayed in my mind.

The morning routine went well, and I was able to observe my first thoughts during meditation and let them pass. *Quit. You don't have to do this. Give up.* The second thoughts made more sense. *What else are you going to do today? Give it a shot.* I had breakfast and performed my next activity, which was to go to the gym. More thoughts came that were hard to navigate, but I hung in there.

After lunch and afternoon meds, it was time to get ready for volunteering. "I just can't believe you are doing this!" my mom was so proud.

I thought back to an old stand-up comedy bit where the comedian said he liked hanging around his grandma because she made him feel strong and special. "Honey, will you bring in the milk? It's so heavy," she said.

"Oh, you mean this?" He hoisted his hand over his head, showing how easy it was for him to lift the carton.

"You are so strong!" she said.

Thoughts of avoidance kicked in on the car ride over, which I handled with a square breathing exercise. I noticed that my anxiety was no worse while waiting in the parking lot to walk in than it was the whole day thinking about this moment, like when my friends didn't really care that I passed on beer a few months ago after agonizing over the conversation all day.

I entered the building and felt vulnerable and insecure. "May I help you?" asked the woman at the front desk.

"Yeah, uh, I'm here for volunteering," I replied.

She barely looked up. "Wait over there, please."

I took a seat in the waiting area until a young woman approached and introduced herself. My social skills were rusty.

"Hey, Brett, thanks for helping us out today. I'm going to give you a tour of the facility now. You'll probably be in the warehouse organizing boxes after that."

She can definitely tell that I was in a psych ward recently. She can definitely tell that I have bipolar. "Uh, okay!" I said a bit loudly, but we moved on.

"Before we get started, I'm going to have you sign in. Wait in line behind the others and fill out the sign-in sheet when you get to the front." I looked up and saw a line of people who were interacting and clearly already knew each other. *Shit.* This was one of those moments where one might expect that in a room full of volunteers, someone would spark up conversation and help me feel comfortable as the new person. But instead, I had a few people eye me up and down as I waited uncomfortably to sign in. I felt nauseated and light-headed waiting in line. *Stay hydrated!* I heard Dr. F's voice in my head, realizing that I had been so caught up in getting here that I overlooked drinking proper amounts of fluids.

I felt panicky with everything that was happening around me, but then I took a deep breath and a glimpse of my old self came back. *Whoa, whoa, whoa. Relax, dude. You are standing in line with a bunch of random people and volunteering your time. You are a little light-headed, so go get a drink. These people aren't intimidating, and if they seem to be, then fuck 'em. You know why you are here, and it's a huge step to be standing in this room right now. You can do this.* I stood up a bit straight and took another deep breath. I worked my way in front of the lady ahead of me in line.

"Hey, how are you?" I asked.

"I'm doing so well. Where are you from?" she replied.

I got more comfortable instantly. "Oh, I'm from the West Hills area, and you?"

"I'm from the North."

"That's cool. Have you ever done this before?"

"Yeah, my husband and I try to come once or twice a week. We are both retired and like giving back." She pointed over to her husband who had already signed in.

"That's cool. I'm Brett." She gave me her name, and then we stood awkwardly for a second for two before I said, "It's nice to meet you!" She said the same. We stood for another second or two awkwardly before she signed in.

There was a line behind me when it was my turn to sign in, and I was struggling with the computer mouse. *Of all things.* I panicked a bit before the woman who was going to give me a tour stepped in and helped me.

"Okay, Brett. You are all set. Follow me and I'll show you what goes on here."

Even though I felt uncomfortable as I followed her to the warehouse, I knew that I was expanding my experiences. On the outside, I showed up, waited in line, said hi, and signed in; but on the inside, I had attempted a double back handspring and came close to sticking the landing. *This is still really hard.*

REMINISCING

Ladies and gentlemen! Welcome to the wonderful world of Systems Fit! I'll be your account executive on this journey of making more money with our state-of-the-art software system that has been fully customized to your gym. I'll take you through a step-by-step process that will have you up and running in no time. "Thank you, Brett. Thank you so much. What would we do without you?"

Ladies and gentlemen! Welcome to the wonderful world of Systems Fit, and congratulations on becoming our newest group of employees. I'll be your implementation manager on this journey of helping gym owners make more money with our state-of-the-art software system that is customized to meet our client's needs. I'll take you through a step-by-step training process that will have you helping customers in no time. "Thank you, Brett. Thank you so much. What would we do without you?"

Ladies and gentlemen! Welcome to the wonderful world of Systems Fit, and congratulations on becoming newly promoted managers! I'll be your manager of client services on this journey of helping your teams provide world-class service to our customers. I'll be here every step of the way in your new manager training. "Thank you, Brett. Thank you so much. What would we do without you?"

Ladies and gentlemen! Welcome to the wonderful world of Systems Fit, and congratulations on becoming newly promoted senior managers! I'll be your director of operations on this journey of helping your managers and their teams provide world-class service to our customers. I'll be here every step of the way in your new senior manager training. "Thank you, Brett. Thank you so much. What would we do without you?"

"Got it, Brett? Dave here is going to put a box on a shelf in this warehouse, and you have to record the spot on this spreadsheet."

I snapped out of my daydream about my last job. "Yep, got it."

For the next two hours I watched an older man named Dave walk over to a pallet, lift a box, find the right place, and store it away. My job was to see the label on the shelf and record it on a spreadsheet. "Maybe next time I'll let you store the boxes and I'll record if you think you can handle it."

"Yeah, I can handle it."

I had mixed emotions about the warehouse. On the one hand, the work was easy, which calmed my nerves and helped me build confidence. On the other hand, it reminded me how far I had fallen in my career. I had been working on so many things internally, dealing with bipolar disorder, that I had lost sight of what it was like out there in the real world.

On my next attempt at the warehouse, I felt less anxious but more aware of my career situation. There was a seventeen-year-old, home for the summer, who was helping Dave and me out.

"Can you guys go any faster?" he asked us in a condescending manner. "We could be getting so much more done if we pick it up a bit. Come on!"

Sure, we're all here to serve you. I thought about how many people I had fired for poor performance and allowed this seventeen-year-old to make me feel bad about mine. Dave was happy to move faster. He was there for the right reasons and welcomed the extra help. I wanted to punch this little shit in the face and take out all my frustration on him. I sat back and kept it under control as this spoiled seventeen had his way with me.

On the same day, the director of the whole operation came down to check on us, and he looked familiar.

"Brett? Is that you?" He looked at me with confusion on his face.

"Hey, Matt." Matt and I went to high school together. He wasn't the most popular and not someone that I would have expected to be several layers of management ahead of me. "Welcome to the team. Thanks for helping out!"

"No problem, Matt." *Good for him.*

When I reported my ego issues back to family and medical professionals, they reminded me why I was there in the first place. They also thought it was noble work to help organize these supplies and boxes to help people that were in need. For some reason, however, I wasn't catching the "helping the world" vibe. I was solely focused on my own progress and becoming impatient. I needed someone to need me. I needed someone to thank me and ask what they would do without me.

BROS TRIP

When Jerry asked if I wanted to take a trip to Denver with him and Russell months ago, I had no choice but to say yes.

"Come on, you'll be fine by then," he said.

Today, I was regretting that decision. Not only would I have to be on point with my medication and routines, but I'd have to do it with a two-hour time difference. *Okay, nine is seven, twelve is ten, and nine is seven.* I packed my things and went with Jerry to the airport; he had driven across the state to travel with me to make sure I was okay with the long journey. Russell would meet us there and the annual bros trip tradition was formed. We decided that we would take turns planning the trip each year and pick a new city to hang out in.

I always liked the window seat because I could rest my head on the side and not have to allow others to come and go to the restroom, but on this trip, I couldn't look out of the window. Every time I did, I was reminded that I was sitting in a chair in the sky. *This is so messed up.* I looked over at Jerry who was sleeping comfortably and gave him a look. *Why did you make me do this?* A few hours later, we landed, and I felt relieved. Denver was a peaceful place and good for my soul.

We met up with Russell at the hotel, and the three musketeers were together again. Jerry took charge. "Okay, guys, I've planned a few things, as I said in those emails. Tomorrow morning, we are going white-water rafting."

What? I should have read those emails instead of just replying "Works for me."

"We have to get up at 5:00 a.m. and drive two hours."

Ugh.

"That should take up most of the day. We'll go hiking tomorrow, and there's a concert at the Red Rocks Amphitheater on the last night. This is gonna be awesome!" Russell was excited but had a sense that this was a lot for me. *One hour at a time.*

I got up at 4:00 a.m. and did my morning routine using my headphones to meditate. I felt a little tired but got good sleep and had an additional two hours because of the time zone change. *Be careful with the sleep! It's one of the main things that can trigger another episode.* My phone buzzed a few minutes later, reminding me to take my afternoon meds with me on the adventure. *If we get stranded out there, I'm screwed.*

The drive was fine, and the rafting was easy. We stopped for lunch, where I was able to pull my afternoon medication out of my life jacket pocket and down the pills with the water provided to us for lunch. I got a slight sense of relief after the afternoon pills were taken. It meant that I wouldn't have to worry about meds until dinner. We had a great evening, and I felt accomplished going to bed that night in the hotel, even though tomorrow's activities would test me just as much.

The next day, we slept in a bit, and I knocked out my morning routine before my brothers were up. We went on a nice long hike through the mountains. It was a relaxing, enjoyable experience, and I felt free for the first time in a long time. Russell was proud of me, and Jerry treated me like he always did, which was a compliment. *He clearly can't tell anything is wrong with me.*

I stuck to my routine on the final day and walked the hundreds of steps to get to the Red Rocks Amphitheater for the reggae show that Jerry had purchased for us. The show was great, although there was weed smoke all around me. My brothers were both aware that inhaling weed could trigger another episode, so they wafted their hands in front of me to block the pathway. *Now that's loyalty.*

When the trip was over, I was satisfied with how I handled myself. Getting away from home and mixing up the routine was healthy. It was very important that I get back in the groove quickly, however. It was clear that my brothers had my back no matter what.

Maybe they didn't fully understand what I was going through. Maybe they weren't that interested in hearing about all the hardest stuff. But I didn't really need them to be.

After the first annual bros trip, I came back home with an extra pep in my step. I was able to be disciplined but also creative with my medication. I handled the time zone change. I flew. *Okay, okay, okay, this bipolar thing may be beatable.*

THE BIG LEAGUES

I'm standing at the whiteboard at the Systems Fit office holding a dry erase marker, dressing business casual, and writing out the steps to perform a successful rollout of the Systems Fit software to one of the largest gym franchises in the world. My three senior managers ask questions, and I answer them all. They leave the room and get to work.

I blinked a few times and found myself sitting on my bed in sweatpants and a T-shirt at my mom's holding a dry erase marker staring at my whiteboard. *Okay, so meds morning, afternoon, and evening have to stay stagnant. No way around those events. But they don't really take any time. All I have to do is make sure I have enough meds on hand. Morning routine needs to be done every day, which takes about an hour, but no need to freak out if it's missed once in a while due to things like vacation. One psychiatry appointment and one therapy appointment each week for an hour each. Working out can be moved around but must be done at least three days a week for about thirty minutes each time. I also need to get at least one article of The Poker Project done per week, which takes two hours, and let's not forget about volunteering twice a week for two hours. And throw Stir Eazy on there as a floater if Russell has time. Also make sure chess is there once a week for three hours.*

I sat back and felt satisfaction for the first time in a long time as I figured out how and when my time would be spent. The foundation of what my schedule needed to be was becoming clear, but my social life was still hurting, and I had not found a true career path.

"Brett! Taylor Swift is performing! Do you want to come down and watch? I have it on," my mom's voice projected up the stairs. *Oh yeah, and I still don't have any sort of independence.*

Hanging out with Sierra was the most comfortable of all my social options. It must have been obvious to her because we started spending more time together. She got me out of the house to play mini golf, we went for long walks, and we'd see movies at the theater. If at any point I was uncomfortable with the people around us or the level of stimulation, then she was happy to abandon plans and head back home.

My dad had extra tickets to an MLB baseball game downtown and offered them up. This would have been a hard no if I didn't have Sierra to go with me. But I accepted the offer and mentally prepared to be around a big crowd of people in a vulnerable place far from home.

I put on a nice shirt and jeans for the first time in a long time. I found some old cologne in the bathroom and pumped a few spays on. *Wow, there you are. It's been a long time.* I looked like my old self and took the short drive to Sierra's. We decided to take public transit, which was a short walk from her house, to avoid having to park downtown. She looked amazing, which gave me more confidence to go on this adventure with her.

Oh shit! It's packed in here. I became anxious as people bumped into us on the crowded train. *Can he handle this? Can Brett handle this?* I experienced a familiar delusion. *Just breathe. No one is talking about you.* I looked over at Sierra, and she wasn't concerned, so I let it pass.

Okay, gate 4, section 2, row L, seat 5. Sierra looked at me like she didn't want to navigate the stadium to find our seats, so I stepped up. *Okay, let's do this.* "Follow me," I said. *Okay, there is gate 5, go left.* A fast-walking man bumped into me. *Thanks!* On the way to section 2, we smelled food, and it took both of our worries away. "Hungry?" I asked. She nodded yes with a big smile on her face. We stood in line together and ate our burgers, standing over a garbage can.

We managed to find the seats and enjoy the game. At one point, the mascot came near us, and we both panicked. *Don't even think about trying to take a picture with us!* Sierra could be outgoing when she wanted to be but was more of an introvert like me as her default.

We were able to enjoy the rest of the game, and while I still felt abnormal anxiety on the ride home, we made it.

Later that night, after a few worry thoughts about my career, I became aware of my new normal. A baseball game had always meant one thing to me my whole life, but now it was different. Now I was aware of what it was like to be living in a world where finding your seat might be a hard thing to do. I still had myself in a disabled category and was frustrated with my situation, but I felt like I could now empathize with others who struggle and stand up with them. I had been through a lot but felt a new motivation to lead by example.

ONE-TO-ONE THOUGHTS

"So I'm feeling a bit better, but I'm paranoid," I said, sitting across from Dr. E.

He gave me a warm smile and replied, "Feeling better. How about that? Tell me more about feeling paranoid."

"Well, I feel like I have to hold back."

"What do you mean by that?" he asked.

"The other day I was driving to the gym timidly, and a Ford pickup truck cut me off. My mood spiked from 0 to 100, and I called him an asshole under my breath. I took a few deep breaths and worried that this might be an unhealthy reaction and that it might put me into another manic episode. I had these unfamiliar feelings before my last episode."

"Ah, I see," he said.

"And on the other end of things, I was kicking ass on the puzzle and getting piece after piece while listening to loud techno music. I felt like I could finish the whole thing and was buzzed off the music. I'm worried that I may have put myself into a manic place doing that. It makes me sad to think that I can't just enjoy things without constantly worrying if it's good or bad for me. It's depressing and exhausting to think this much about every emotion."

Dr. E put his pencil down as usual and sat back in his chair. "Brett, you cannot think yourself into another manic episode. The fact that you are aware enough to describe vividly what you are experiencing is a very good sign. It shows that you have an understanding of what your triggers are. Every person gets angry and excited, and you are no different. Will you ever know with 100 percent certainty that you will not have another episode? No, you will not. But I don't know one person that can be 100 percent certain about most things in life."

There's that cliché nobody-can-know-everything answer that everyone tells me. "Okay, I've worked on accepting all that, but my thoughts are very intense, and they feel uncomfortable. It can have a hold on me."

"Brett, what's a recent pleasant thought that you've had?" he asked.

"Uh, going for a walk with Sierra?" I answered.

"Okay, and what's a recent challenging thought that you've had?"

"That I would never get over this feeling of uncertainty and have to question every thought and emotion I have for the rest of my life."

"Okay, Brett, those are good examples. Now you are a math guy. I want you to understand that every thought is a one. No thought is greater than another because they are all just thoughts! So both of the previous thoughts that you described are worth one. They are worth the same amount of pull. All thoughts are one-to-one. Does that make sense?" he asked.

I pictured rolling dice and made the connection that no matter what number they landed on, they were both still the same size and shape. "Yes, it does." *I'm still not satisfied.*

"But it still feels out of my control when the harder thoughts come in. For example, I'll get caught in a loop: I live at home with no job, but I'm too afraid to get a real job. And why am I afraid to get a real job? Because I have bipolar disorder. And bipolar disorder is never going away, so I'll be living at home with no job forever. The cycle continues, and I get anxious."

"That sounds like a tough cycle, but look at what you are doing. You are making your entire world about that cycle at that moment. When you are volunteering, are you having these thoughts?"

"Not usually."

"And how about when you are with Sierra? Working out? Playing chess?"

"Well, no," I answered.

"Right. Your world is bigger than the moment you are in. That thing that you do with the loop might just be hardwired in. The second thought might be to understand that you are making your world very small when caught up in the cycle. Make sense?"

I'm going to use that one. "Yes, makes sense."

"Okay, one more thing. I have to confess that I missed a dose of medicine the other day, and it scared me as well. I was caught up in my routine and forgot to bring it with me for lunch. By the time I got home that night, it was too late. I called Dr. F in somewhat of a panic and took a little extra time the following day to recalibrate. She said it was okay, but I couldn't stop thinking about how I was so careless. How can I even trust myself?"

He smiled and laughed for a second. "Brett, you are a very responsible person, and you have every reason to trust yourself. Mistakes will happen, but again, you've alerted the proper channels and learned from your mistakes no matter how big or small they may be."

On the drive home, I felt that we had accomplished a lot in that session, and I was armed with a few more tools to manage some of these uncomfortable thoughts that were entering my mind. When I got home, my mom asked me how the session went.

"Fine," I said.

THE TRACK

The track at my local high school was empty on this sunny, hot day. *Just me and the track.* I approached the turf wearing a cutoff T-shirt, Nike basketball shorts, low-cut socks, and Under Armour running shoes with my wireless headphones, playing the newest Eminem album at a reasonably high volume. *I cannot think myself into a manic episode.* I felt strong and free after letting my last therapy session settle in. *All thoughts have equal value.* I scanned the full area and took note of the steep concrete hill and the bleachers that they led to. I checked my phone and confirmed my workout that was scheduled to take place. I thought about the bottle of water that I chugged before driving over and took note of the water fountain close by. I had eggs and oatmeal a few hours ago for breakfast. *Fully prepared. Feeling good today. The stars are aligned today. Well, wait, I did most of this stuff. It wasn't blind luck.*

I placed my car keys on the side of the track. *Okay, one time around as a warm-up. Then just have fun with it and see what happens.* I started jogging. *My breathing feels on point today.* I passed the concrete hill. *I'm going to sprint up that son of a bitch today.* I continued to jog. *This straightaway is prime for an all-out sprint.* I turned the corner into the semicircle. *Might need a break here at some point. Sit-ups?* I continued around the half circle and became fixated on the bleachers. I *should run up and do those too.* I finished the warm-up lap. *Okay, it's go time.*

I picked up the pace around the first half circle and approached the concrete hill. I swung my arms and pressed my feet on the concrete, shooting my body up the hill. *Wooo! I'm still the same person.*

Let's go! I trotted back down the hill and got back on the track for the straightaway. *All-out sprint.* I charged forward and kept my breathing steady, feeling no pain until I reached the second semicircle. I got on the ground and did ten sit-ups before hopping up and running around to the bleachers. I slammed my feet on each step and trotted back down. *I am still strong.* I made it back to the track for the final sprint and moved like lightning on the last straightaway. *Do some push-ups.* I knocked out ten push-ups and stood up. *That's round 1. Go again.*

I felt an emotional tear falling down my cheek as I approached the concrete hill on this round. Russell was on my right, and Jerry was on my left. *This hill is bipolar, and we're about to smash it!* They disappeared. I sprinted up faster on this round and trotted back to the track. A group of men from the pizza shop in Texas were standing in my way, but I wasted no time moving into the all-out sprint and flying through them. They disappeared. I knocked out the sit-ups fast and noticed a face forming in the clouds. *Breathe in. Breathe out.* It disappeared. *I got this.* I stood back up and approached the bleachers for the second time, slamming my feet on each step and noticing that the world was not shifting back and forth like it had before. *That was scary. This is normal.*

As I approached the final sprint on this round, I pictured a slingshot waiting for me on the track. *I'm allowed to find creative ways to motivate myself. That's something special about me, not something to worry about.* I stepped on the slingshot, and my surroundings went blurry as I darted down the straightaway. *Finish strong. Go until you can't anymore.* I got down in a push-up position and started cranking out push-ups. *Don't stop.* I thought about the pain that my mental health issues had caused me over the last decade. The straitjacket. The Taser. A razor blade from the bathtub. *Don't stop.* I was back in my room at the psych ward pushing until I couldn't go anymore. *Don't stop.* I decided that I could beat this thing and whatever happened, happened; I decided that I already won. *Stop.* I lay on my back and looked at the clouds, not seeing any faces and thinking about how I had sobbed alone in my room on the psych ward after a similar push-up work out. I smiled and took a deep breath.

I savored the moment and eventually rolled up, got my keys, and drove home. *But you only went around twice. Stop. But this still doesn't change anything. I guess. Where are you living again? At my mom's. Have you been able to hold down a full-time job yet? Not yet. Why don't you drink? It's not good for me. Are you an alcoholic? No. Well, why isn't it good for you? I'm on a pill that doesn't mix well with alcohol. What's the pill for? It helps with my moods. Moods? Yes. Is everything okay? Yes. Do you drink coffee? Decaf. Energy drinks? No. Well, why did you move home? I was changing jobs.* My mental workout was just as challenging on the drive home.

MEAL PREP

I was able to string together a number of good days in a row. Part of what shifted my attitude from negative and hopeless to positive and hopeful was having something to do that I enjoyed planned for some time in the future. That activity could have been chess, a movie with a friend, or The Poker Project. It really didn't matter. It was more the peace of mind that I had value in some way and that a future event might actually be enjoyable. I still had a tendency to get down on myself often and had many bad days but was reminded by my mom to look at a full week instead of one isolated day to measure progress. When I reflected in this way, it was clear that I was having many more good days than bad ones overall.

I wasn't fully up and running yet by any means, but I was beginning to do more activities on my own. I began coming and going at my mom's rather than stuck on the couch all day afraid of the world. *Okay, morning routine: take meds to go, workout, doctor's appointment, chess, Sierra, go!* I was adjusting to this new life of mine, this healthy life. *I'm feeling better now than I did before I had bipolar.* After a few weeks of owning my time and my illness, I thought more about what it would take to become independent.

"Dinner!" my mom called from the other room.

"Okay, coming down!" It hit me that in order for me to become independent, I would have to be able to feed myself and not Chick-fil-A for every meal.

"So, Mom," I said while scooping rice onto my plate from a bowl, "I'm thinking I'm going to start making healthy meals for myself. You can have some if you want too. How cool would it be if

I could take care of all that and not have to bother you as much?" I saw a sparkle in her eye showing how proud she was of me but then a nervous smile at the realization that her baby was pushing to get back out into the dangerous real world again.

"I can't believe my ears! That's a great idea. Do not worry about me. Get yourself in order. I'll be fine," she replied.

I had been around enough healthy people between my childhood of basketball and working at a gym as an adult to know what I should and should not be eating. I had never needed to be this disciplined or structured in the past, however. *Eggs, fruit, oatmeal for breakfast. Turkey wrap for lunch. Chicken or salmon, veggies, and rice for dinner.* I decided I would change out dipping sauce for chicken at night to give it some variety. Not the most exciting of lineups, but it would work because it was simple and doable.

I gripped the handlebars on my cart and pushed through the sliding doors into the vegetable section at the supermarket. *Peppers, onion, broccoli, zucchini.* I couldn't get the plastic bag to open, and my hands started shaking. *Thanks a lot, lithium.* I put the raw veggies in my cart and did the same with apples and bananas. I strolled through more of the store toward the prepackaged chicken. *Breathe in. Breathe out. Breathe in. Breathe out.* I knew my mom had enough Tupperware for at least twelve meals, so I got four twelve-packs of raw chicken tenders. *Off to get the eggs!* It felt great to be living in reality in a public place. I picked up an eighteen-pack of eggs and headed to check out because I knew there was oatmeal, sauces, and cold cuts at home. All the self-checkout counters were open, but I decided to wait in line and relieve some of the pressure of figuring it out. *Figure that one out later.*

I made it home. *Honey, I'm home! Oh wait. Mom, I'm home!*

She was so proud of me. "I don't ever remember you cooking before!" I gave her that one and didn't defend myself. I was in too good of a mood from getting a taste of my independence back.

Two hours later, there were twelve Tupperware containers laid out, each with four grilled chicken tenders, veggies, and rice. I took one of the containers and ate it, not focusing on the dull taste but more on the fact that it was fuel for my body.

"This is the best chicken I've ever tasted!" my mom said as she stole a tender from one of the containers.

"Oh please, now I know you are full of shit," I replied playfully.

I stacked the other eleven meals and stored them in the downstairs fridge. Then it was just the two of us standing around the puzzle after sharing a light-hearted moment of cooking. There was a special underlying feeling in the room that we were making progress and crawling out of the hell of this past year. Neither of us said a word.

THE NEW NORMAL

This is bipolar disorder. I had just finished another weekly workout at the track on a warm day and decided to turn off the headphones and walk a few laps. *This is bipolar disorder.* These words now came with less fear and more curiosity. *Did I really almost jump off a bridge in Texas? Did I really yell at the top of my lungs at a crowd of people in public?* I laughed to myself nervously and kept walking. *But look, I'm outside on a nice day feeling good. I'm okay. I know what I have to do to manage this thing. Yes, I'm scared that I could have another episode. Yes, I'm afraid that I don't have a career yet. But honestly, I feel better. Maybe even better than before I had my episodes. Maybe my life wasn't so perfect back then either.* My mood turned for a second and boosted my confidence. *And you know what else? If anyone doesn't like it, then I don't really give a shit.* I decided that having bipolar was part of who I was, and I had always liked who I was. *This is special, not a disability.*

I walked through a day of the "perfect" life that I used to have in my mind. *I used to wake up. Eat breakfast. Take a shower. Go to work. Come home and work out. Work some more at home. Have a drink and dinner. Go to bed.* And what did I do now? *Wake up. Eat breakfast. Take a shower. Work on projects. Work out. Have dinner. Go to bed. Yes, there's a few other bullshit things but not too far off. So maybe I can have a good life and have bipolar. Maybe I can do things that I never would have done if I were not bipolar.* I was excited to see how this would all play out.

Russell called, "So tell me a little bit about what it's like now."

I hadn't really been asked that question by anyone except my mom and doctors. "Well, Russ, uh. It's pretty much the same as before. I have to take some time to see doctors, and I still have no clue what I'm going to do for work, but generally, I just have to live a healthy lifestyle and take my meds," I explained.

Russell could totally get behind the idea of a healthy lifestyle because he had one himself. He was always very aware of his diet and worked out regularly. "I don't even like alcohol that much anymore, dude. It's stupid and makes me feel like shit," he said.

"Yeah, honestly, I don't even miss it that much. I'm getting used to decaf coffee also. Nothing special, but it's fine."

"That's really good. Have you thought about what you want to do once you get all this figured out?"

"Yeah, a little bit. My mind is in a good place right now, but I haven't been tested that much. I'm thinking about trying out a chess league downtown. It will be a much bigger challenge than playing in a small room at the library."

"Wow, that's awesome. Will you be the best one there?" he asked.

"Absolutely not. I heard one of the old guys at my club talking about how there are grandmasters there."

"What's a grandmaster?" he asked.

"Someone who is grand at chess."

"Ha ha. Well, they've never seen you before."

"Chess doesn't really work like that, but thanks."

"Keep pushing, B. You are doing awesome."

"Thanks."

The puzzle looked different that night. It wasn't some masterpiece that I had to complete in order to prove something or receive some sort of accolade. No, it was just a big puzzle taking up a large amount of space on the dining room table, an old activity that was valuable at taking up time when I needed it to be. Now the puzzle was much smaller because my world felt bigger. The whole house felt different. TVs and radios were nothing to be afraid of, reflections and glares didn't have hidden meaning, and my internal thoughts were more of a whisper than loud roar.

I knew it was time to start cleaning up the puzzle. I was nowhere near done, but I realized that finishing it was never the most important thing. I made a healthy connection that bipolar disorder could be seen in the same way. I could do what I had to do without an end game in mind. I could treat it like a never-ending project that could constantly be improved and updated based on the climate of my life. There was no finish line. I finally understood what my doctors meant when they said that living with bipolar disorder was a marathon, not a sprint. I came to the conclusion that I could still enjoy the run, even without competition or a finish line on the track. It was this mindset that helped take my recovery into a new phase of getting back out there and living my life.

BACK TO CLASS

"Real estate might suit you well," said Dr. F at my next appointment. "There is a period of classroom learning before taking a test to become licensed. Licensed real estate agents have flexible hours, which will be good for you. You'll be able to schedule time for self-care tasks and build a career."

Dr. F and I were trying to get me into a new job situation, which was why we started with volunteering, doing a task in a meaningful, social situation. Then moving along, we thought of a training program aiming toward a real job as an option. That was how the idea of real estate came up. First, volunteer to train my brain to do a meaningful task. Then put my brain in a learning situation that required reading and testing, with the idea that at the end of the program, I'd be trained to do a job that wasn't just an entry-level position, which was my fear of starting all over again with a job. Her other recommendations had been spot-on up to this point, and I had no reason to believe that this would be any different.

After some research online, I learned that I'd have to do sixty hours of coursework in a live classroom or online, followed by the state and national exams. After passing the exams would I affiliate with a brokerage and be able to start practicing as an officially licensed real estate agent. I chose to push myself and do the sixty hours in a live classroom setting. It was another opportunity to train my brain while also being in a social environment. I submitted my application, purchased the class materials, and had a date scheduled for my first class.

I had a blast telling everyone that I had signed up to become a real estate agent, but in the back of my mind, I was terribly anxious. *Is this normal anxiety or unhealthy anxiety? Probably normal.* When the first night of class came around, I was determined to take care of business, but I was vulnerable and uncomfortable. The class was three times a week from 6:00 p.m. to 9:00 p.m. I got in the car and headed out for this new adventure.

I showed up forty-five minutes early and was the first one there.

"Can I help you?" a nice woman asked as I walked in the small waiting area outside what looked like a classroom.

"Yes, uh, I'm looking for the real estate class?" I choked out.

"Hmm, well, this isn't a real estate class. Are you sure you have the right office?" I was embarrassed and checked my phone.

"I thought so. I'll look around." I walked out without asking her for help. *Shit, where the hell am I? Why am I doing this? I should just go home now. I can't do this.* I observed my first thoughts. *Breathe in. Breathe out. You are so early, take your time, and confirm the address. It's all good.* I looked back at my phone and noticed that I had two of the numbers switched. I found the room still thirty minutes early and still the first one there.

"Hi, I'm Brett Stevens. Here for the real estate class." I was still timid but proud of myself for making it through the door. *Please let this be the right place.*

"Hey, Brett! Let me just check you off my list here. Oh, there you are! Welcome. You are the first one here, so take these books and have a seat in the classroom. Others will be arriving shortly." I said thank you and found a seat in the back corner of the room. *Hidden in the back of the class seems reasonable.*

There were about six rows of white tables in front of me and a long whiteboard covered the width of the wall in front of the class. *Now that's a whiteboard!* Then people of all shapes, sizes, and ages started trickling in and taking their seats. Some were friendly, and others looked tired and disinterested. I gave awkward nods to anyone who came in my line of site. *If they only knew I was bipolar, then they would be amazed that I was here. But why would I care either way?* My mind wondered about new topics that I had never considered before my diagnosis. I couldn't help but be jealous of every person that entered the room. *She looks like she has a nice family at home. He's just out of college getting his career started early. The two friends in the front might just be learning as a hobby.* I had the whole room mapped out as I sat in the back corner quietly.

Then a friendly middle-aged woman sat next to me and took a deep sigh as she placed her materials on the desk. "Great time for a real estate class," she said sarcastically while looking at me with a smile. "My husband is at work, kids are running around with their friends doing God knows what, and I'm here sitting with people half my age trying to learn how to sell a house."

"Ha ha, how do you know I'm half your age?" I asked.

"You are a baby face. Give me a break," she replied.

"I'm Christine." She put her hand out.

"Brett," I said.

Christine asked me easy questions for the next few minutes that I was comfortable answering. She gave me a slight boost in confidence without knowing it. Then the door of the classroom closed and a bald, clean-cut three-hundred-pound older man wearing an expensive suit trotted in, holding too many binders and papers. He let out a sigh of relief as he dropped his belongings on the table at the head of the class.

"Open your textbooks to page 1," he said forcefully. "We'll start right away, and this will not be as easy as everyone says it is." I did as he said and was anxious to see if my bipolar brain was still capable of learning new things.

STILL GOT IT

I'm at college in the South, sitting in the back of the class with my biology professor teaching about the theory of evolution. Every one of his words is directed at me, and the entire lecture hall turns around to get a glance at the one who is going to save the world. I sit back comfortably and confident, knowing that I have the special powers necessary to do it and that God is on my side. I blink a few times.

"Your homework for next class is to read pages 20–50 in the textbook on the topics of ethics and contracts." I came back from my memory trip. "Then you must complete the workbook sections on those chapters which are indicated in the textbook." Mr. H had finished the three-hour lecture and gave us homework before letting us leave. *Feels pretty similar to any other school I've had in my life.* I wondered if I would be able to focus long enough to complete the homework before the next class.

My schedule was really filling up, so I decided to end volunteering at the warehouse and use that time to study for real estate. I chose to study at the library because I was comfortable there, after playing chess a number of times and working on The Poker Project often. I opened the thick textbook and turned to page 20.

"A fiduciary duty is the obligation to act in the best interest of your client," it read. *A fiduciary duty is the obligation to act*—fiduciary *is a weird word. Weird word. Don't they call that alliteration? Pay attention! A fiduciary*—*fairy is inside of the word fiduciary somewhere. How cool. Focus! A fiduciary duty is the obligation to act in the best interest of your client. So it's kind of like how a lawyer represents their client. Same thing with a real estate agent.* It was not easy to get through the thirty pages of text and workbook assignments, but ten bathroom breaks and two hours later, I was done.

I felt accomplished leaving the library, like I had just expanded my skills. *I could barely read a year ago!* The small success at the library did not make me any less anxious in the class that night. Someone was sitting in my seat in the back, so I had to sit closer to the front.

"What is a fiduciary duty?" Mr. H asked.

I looked around, and no one was raising their hand. *Fuck it.* I raised my hand for the first time with bipolar disorder. "A fiduciary duty is the obligation to act in the best interest of your client," I said, somewhat confidently.

"Very good, Brett," he said. "Can anyone give us an example?" he asked the room while scanning his head.

I raised my hand again. "Would it be kind of how a lawyer represents his or her client?"

"That will work," he said. "Someone clearly did the reading." Then we went on to the next topic.

That felt good. I worked hard in class for the next two months and passed the final exam, finishing in the top 5 of the class. *I'm still the same.*

I was sure that it was normal anxiety that I had on the drive to take the national and state real estate exams. *I was nervous before the SATs, and I'm nervous now. No big deal.* Everyone at the test site was friendly, and I was able to take care of business, passing in the ninetieth percentile. I was officially ready to be a real estate agent and affiliate with a brokerage.

On the drive to the affiliate, I reflected on what it took to get to this moment. I thought about how the last decade of my life had been a blur of success in the real world, with three bouts of mania, hospitalizations, anxiety, and depression. I had accomplished so much in my recovery that walking in for the interview was easy.

"So, Brett, tell me a little about yourself," asked the manager, as I sat across from him. *Where do I even start?*

"Well, I'm from the area, and I live right up the road. I am working on a few projects but plan on making real estate my main focus," I continued, noticing my thoughts coming and going as I answered.

"I was the captain of the basketball team." *Before I almost killed myself speeding on the highway in college.* "I was a full-time online professional poker player for a period of time." *Before walking on cars and getting beat up by cops.* "I worked for a start-up company in Texas and grew the team from two employees to thirty-five employees." *Before almost jumping off a bridge.*

"Wow, Brett, that's very impressive, and I'm sure you will do well here."

After the meeting, I was officially a licensed real estate agent. I regrouped at home base and took note of the whiteboard, noticing my full week filled with healthy activities and now a new career. My first thought was that I needed to show others in my situation how I was able to build my life back.

CROSSOVER

"You know I've been beaten up by cops and put in handcuffs before," I said casually to my mom and her boyfriend sitting around the dining room table while eating dinner.

He looked at me like I was crazy. "You have? You are so calm and cool all of the time. What happened?"

"Well, I was in one of my manic episodes and was frustrated and walking on cars downtown. Finally, someone called the cops, and they took me to the psych ward."

He looked astonished. "Really?"

"Yeah, I have a bunch of stories like that. Weird things that happened while I was sick."

"I knew you had some issues but didn't realize things like that happened. You should write about it. Start from when you were a child."

"Maybe I will," I replied.

His reaction was so strong, and I had gotten comfortable writing for The Poker Project that it seemed reasonable to start writing about some of my experiences with bipolar disorder. Dr. F thought it was a great idea and would be therapeutic, so I started writing.

I was sitting alone at the dining room table, and it was quiet, except for a bird chirping through the window. *Where do I even begin?* I opened up my laptop and created a Google Doc and stared blankly for a few minutes. The bird chirping outside reminded me of the weird relationship I had with them in college during my first episode. I wrote "Birds" on the blank doc. *That will be cool to write about, but you have to start from the beginning.* I sat back in my chair and could only recall memories having to do with basketball. *Okay, write about the most prominent moments in basketball first.*

I took a deep breath and placed myself in a scene that I remembered vividly, including the music that was playing and the tastes, sounds, and smells that were present many years ago. I started typing very fast, and when I looked up thirty minutes later, I had written a full page about an old basketball camp experience. *That wasn't so bad.* I kept my schedule in mind and my doctor's voices that echoed "Pace yourself. Do not get obsessed with work." I decided that I would write one section a week and see if I could continue to build the story of my life.

As the weeks went by, I started to enjoy the writing experience more and more. It felt like I was reliving some of the highlights of my childhood, like meeting Michael Jordan and playing varsity basketball. I knew that when my development approached college, that the story would get more serious. I was also searching for signs during my childhood of bipolar disorder. *Did I miss something back then?*

When the basketball writing was over, I decided to go back and write about personal events in my life, weaving them in between the basketball stories. *I did win Camper of the Year, didn't I?* I laughed as I reflected on the biggest award there was back in the day. Writing about hitting puberty and going on family vacation was fun as well. The story was rounding out as I developed my character all the way to graduating high school. I'd send the sections to Sierra, my mom, and Russell as I wrote them and was motivated to keep going by their responses.

The first hard section that I had to write was when my dad left. I knew I had to put it in there because it took a toll on my emotional state, and it occurred right before my first episode. It was an important factor in understanding how my mood could change so drastically. The story was fun and relatively light up to that section. I did everything I could to represent myself accurately about how my mind worked and why I was the way that I was.

I had about twenty-five sections written, which would be about seventy pages in a real book and was proud of that. I knew that the rest of the book would be intense and shocking to most of the people who knew me. I also realized that I had been holding these stories in for the past decade. It wasn't anyone's fault, but I really had no reason to bring them up or go into great detail about what happened and why. Based on how I had recalled the first seventy pages of the book through basketball and my personal life, I was sure that I would be able to tell my bipolar story with great accuracy and detail. I would be able to let my friends, family, and whoever else cared in on what I had experienced. I felt good about the amount of writing that I had done but was unsure if it was up to par. I had no previous experience with all this except the short articles that I had written for The Poker Project. *Well, let's give this a shot.* I opened a new doc and wrote in bold at the top, "Birds."

THE STIGMA

I continued to explore the four corners of my mind and work on the book in a consistent fashion over the next few weeks. I came back from training for real estate one day, and my mom was devastated, standing in front of the TV.

"Come watch this, Brett!"

I put my laptop bag down and walked toward her. "Here is a live shot of students evacuating Parkland High School in Daytona Beach, Florida. There is an active shooter on campus," reported the man on TV.

"Wow, I said." They kept the camera on the live action while a roundtable discussion was happening on the other half of the screen.

"This has to be a case of mental illness," said one woman.

"I couldn't agree more. Why would anyone do this?" said a man.

Hey, that's me! I'm mentally ill. "Hey, Mom," I said.

"Yes?"

"I think that's kind of messed up that they would say that. I'm mentally ill. Are you afraid that I'm going to shoot up a school?"

We both realized at the same time that I was in this category now. The category of people who couldn't purchase firearms or go to the military. The category of people who couldn't be trusted. *Let's go compete at something and see who is mentally ill.* I became defensive and felt a surge of adrenaline. But I laughed it off and realized that every day that I lived my life under control, productive, and healthy was another day that I was breaking the stigma.

I had returned Karen's car and purchased a Subaru Legacy awhile back and was feeling supremely independent. I had my life in order. *Morning routine, meds, diet, workouts, hobbies, career, relationships, car, and an understanding of how to balance my life. I can do this.* After eighteen months of recovery, it was time for me to look for my own apartment. I didn't receive any pushback from my mom or doctors because they could see how responsible I was. They were proud of me.

Sierra and I were not officially together when I moved out, which meant I was a single, independent man living on my own with bipolar disorder. After getting moved in, I had to take a second to feel good about my situation. I was convinced that all people who lived with bipolar disorder could do what I did. I became frustrated thinking about individuals who were unhappy with their current situation but still didn't take their meds, didn't trust doctors, or use drugs and alcohol. *I did it. Why can't you?* I had no awareness that not everyone could crash at their moms for eighteen months and have everything taken care of for them like I did.

I adjusted to my morning routine in my new place and found a shared coworking space to work on my writing and real estate stuff. It was nice to be around other people instead of being isolated and working at home. I set up a few blind dates, which were interesting.

"Let's grab a drink. Oh, you don't drink? Why not?" one woman asked me.

"Oh, well, I just don't really like it."

"Really? Did you ever drink?"

"Yeah, I used to."

"Oh, were you an alcoholic or something?"

I scoffed, "No." And that was the end of that. Most of my dates went this way, and I decided that not drinking was a problem. It wasn't that I felt tempted or that I needed to have a drink, but it was the awkward exchange of having to explain why I didn't drink. On some dates, I was asked so many questions about it that I eventually told her that I was bipolar. Which was honest but unnecessary.

But overtime, I became more confident and realized that the people who were so caught up on why I didn't drink were not the people I wanted to be around. My friends from high school still drank, but I was comfortable around them because they didn't care at all about my drinking situation. I never expected the easy part with all this to be giving up was alcohol. It was the social stigma around it that was most difficult.

I found many activities that I preferred doing over drinking, like going to the downtown college basketball games, seeing movies, and watching live music or a comedy show. My life was becoming more normal even with bipolar disorder. Sure, I didn't drink caffeine or alcohol anymore. Sure, I didn't stay out all night. Sure, I was tied to my calendar and required to do breathing exercises and take meds every day. But at the end of all this, I felt like myself, and I wanted to enjoy every minute of that.

HELPING OTHERS

"Brett, this is unbelievable!" said Dr. F in her office during our appointment.

"It is?" I replied, surprised that she was having such a strong reaction.

"Yes, this can help a lot of people."

"Cool!" Dr. F had read my finished manuscript and was pleased.

"With your permission, I'm going to pass the finished version along to some of my colleagues. I'm sure they will find the value in it."

"What is so valuable about it?" I asked.

"Well, it gives the reader firsthand perspective on your episodes. Most books have medical language that makes it hard to get through. This will bridge the gap. For example, it's much easier for me to have a patient look at the 'Bird' section in your book to explain something like mania instead of telling them the definition."

"Very cool."

"I also think you may have a condition called hypermnesia," she said. "You should look it up. It's the incredible ability to remember the details of life events vividly, even during times of trauma. That is clearly what you've done with your writing."

"Sweet," I said.

The book was complete, and I had some great feedback from a medical professional. *Hmm, what could I do with this?* The obvious answer was to try and get it published. I thought about how I would read each section to my mom after it was done, and she would be blown away by some of the detail and be emotional about all the things that I was writing about. I passed the manuscript around to some close friends and family. Some read it instantly and called me in shock about my story. "I had no idea, dude." "I can't believe that happened to you!" "It's amazing how you recovered so many times!" Others didn't get back to me for a while. "Sorry, I was so busy, but I didn't expect it to be like that!" And then others never got back to me. *All good, all good. I don't know what I would do if someone dumped a book on me like that.*

I researched literary agents for a few months and submitted the manuscript to many with no reply. I didn't feel upset because I was already winning based on the reactions I received from friends and family. Finally, I found a vanity publishing company that accepted my work. The book was going to be published.

Brainstorm, Puzzled, and others were on my list for a title, but none of them felt right. Eventually, my attention went to words having to do with basketball, and *Crossover* was the obvious choice. *Crossover dribble in basketball. Crossover moods in bipolar.* Russell and my mom had the idea to have a picture of basketball shoes on the cover without laces, which I liked. Laces were not allowed on the psych ward units because they could be used to harm oneself or others. I liked the symbolism.

The publishing process was torturous. If one word or piece of punctuation was off, it could be weeks for it to be reviewed and updated. The cover design was the same, taking an additional month for what seemed like one small edit. But finally, after months and months of waiting with small amounts of work in between, *Crossover: A Look Inside a Manic Mind* was published.

"Wow, you are a published author now? That's insane. No pun intended," said Jerry as he called to congratulate me on the book being released. I received many calls over the next few weeks with a similar feeling of accomplishment. I was able to feel accomplished as well and didn't instantly ask about what's next, as I would have before being diagnosed with my illness.

I sold a couple hundred copies and received many five-star reviews on Amazon the first week that it was out, which I was very happy about. I didn't have a marketing plan formed but decided that I would figure it out as I went.

"Can you believe that the book is out?" I asked my mom over the phone from my apartment.

"No! It's unbelievable!"

"You know, a lot of people are asking me if you are writing a book. They want to see your perspective in dealing with all this stuff."

"I'm thinking about it. I will get back to you. Not all of us are as determined as you are," she said playfully.

When the publishing company shipped me my first twenty copies of the book, I felt great. The first thing I did was kick back on the couch and start reading.

REFLECTIONS

My life felt normal again, but the three medication doses through-out the day were a constant reminder that I was a person living with bipolar disorder. While my body had developed checks and balances to ensure that I was getting enough sleep, working out, and avoiding isolation, there were still many deeper layers that I had not experi-enced yet as a person with the chronic illness.

I was proactive and got a flu shot one afternoon, as advised by my brother Russell, which went smoothly. I thought the needle going into my arm was cute compared to the constant blood work and tests that were done two years ago when I was first diagnosed. Most things like this felt easy for me after overcoming the traumatic events of my past. I looked at things differently and noticed how minor issues for me might be major issues for someone else, like not getting their dream job or getting dumped by their significant other. Making these observations made me feel strong and reminded me that disabled people have a lot to be proud of.

My throat became sore the next day, and I treated it like I always would have before my illness by drinking lots of water and attempt-ing to get a good night sleep. The following morning, I woke up feeling the old hell-like buzz. *What's going on? I thought I was done with this.* In the past, I would have pushed through this morning slump and chalked it up to having the flu. But today, I was having similar thoughts and feelings to the first day that I came home. *This is your illness coming back. Don't think you will escape. On any random day, you can wake up with these types of thoughts and feelings.* Instead of doing my morning routine, I stayed in bed. I looked at the events on my calendar and canceled them all. I wanted badly to skip my medication, but then a beam of hope came with the "One hundred percent of people with bipolar disorder who do not take their meds will have future episodes" message.

I started having suicidal thoughts. *All this work and learning, to randomly feel depressed? I don't think I'll ever get better. What's the point of all this? If I ended it right now, no one would give a shit.* Thankfully, I had a doctor's appointment the following day with Dr. F and felt the urge to tell her instead of canceling the appointment like I had all others while feeling this way.

"Dr. F, I feel like shit. I don't know what's going on."

She asked a few questions after her initial, "Are you staying hydrated?" one that she usually opened up with when I wasn't feeling well.

"Yeah, I think I have the flu or something, but it's going way beyond that. I'm really depressed."

"Brett, remember what Dr. E asks you often? What is your job?"

"My job is to do what's on my calendar," I replied.

"That's right. So even if you feel unwell, it will not help to cancel everything you have planned and be alone in your apartment all week. That can certainly make it worse."

What she said made sense, and my main takeaway was not to give up on everything when I got sick. Of course, I could cancel certain events and move others around, but being alone with my thoughts was not a good strategy. I learned something by getting the flu as a person with bipolar disorder.

On other occasions, I would get extremely excited about a new idea. *Maybe I could coach basketball. It shouldn't be too hard. Start as a sixth-grade coach, then high school, then college, then NBA, then USA! I'll be coaching Lebron James in no time!* I'd catch myself in the midst of my fast-moving thoughts, breathing fast and with anxiety. Dr. E would reassure me again that I could not think myself into another manic episode, but to make my life about one line of thinking would mean that my life was very small. No one thought should take over my entire life.

They call bipolar a chronic illness because there is no cure. I think of it more as a never-ending project. Even after rebuilding my life and doing certain tasks every day, I'm still learning as new situations come up, like getting the flu or getting caught up in a new idea. I asked myself often, *Is this normal or is this part of bipolar disorder?* After a few cycles, I learned that the flu is still the flu, and a new idea is still a new idea.

SECOND BOOK

Crossover detailed my experiences from childhood to getting to a manageable place with bipolar disorder, and I was satisfied with the response from individuals and family members of individuals with the illness. But it felt like I had left a lot on the table in terms of recovery and building one's life back. With Dr. F's recommendation, I decided that a second book honing in more on my recovery might provide additional value. The information and stories came pouring out as I wrote *Crossover*, and I expected the same for the second book. I sat down and attempted to write the opening. *Okay, let's give this a shot.*

Tough Love

You have been granted a gift. Don't roll your eyes. It's true. You are part of a small segment of the population whose brain works in a different way, arguably an elite way. You have endless potential.

Being diagnosed with bipolar is not your biggest problem. You are your biggest problem. Think about the controllable actions that you take every day. Are they selfish? Lazy? Helping? In your journey with managing bipolar, you will encounter many people that will tell you how great you are doing, how strong you are, and how hard it must be to have drawn the short straw with your mental health. I'm here to tell you that you must meet this thing head-on and own it in order to find whatever

*it is that you have been searching for. No more feel-
ing bad for yourself and making excuses. It's time to
hold yourself accountable and realize that if you are
not doing every possible controllable thing to help
yourself, then it's on you.*

I didn't like that one, so I tried another. *That's garbage. You
sound condescending. Try another.*

Taming the Beast: How to Manage Bipolar Disorder

> *You are responsible for taking care of a
> fire-breathing dragon for the rest of your life. You
> didn't have a say in how or why you've acquired
> the beast, but it's here, following you around. Your
> dragon can be your most valuable asset but also your
> biggest crutch. You must embrace your new compan-
> ion and learn how to leverage it for good, all while
> staying safe.*
>
> *Bipolar disorder itself is as mysterious as a
> fire-breathing dragon. Sometimes you are larger
> than life, flapping your wings and soaring through
> the air, while in other instances you are breathing
> fire all around you, trapped with no place to escape.
> Because each individual experiences bipolar disorder
> in a unique way, everything in between also exists,
> some cases moving from elevated moods to depressed
> moods rapidly, and others staying in these states for
> longer periods of time.*
>
> *Also interesting is what happens within manic
> and depressive states. For example, one person's
> mania may tell him that he is Jesus Christ, while
> others may tell her that she is a Russian spy. On the
> other end of the spectrum, some people take their
> depressive states all the way to suicide, while oth-*

ers climb out of the darkness and find comfort once again.

> *You are unique but also fall under a larger umbrella of mentally ill and then bipolar I or bipolar II. For this reason, I can hand off some tangible skills that will help you tame the best. Just like your dragon, your acquired skills will become unique to you.*

I wasn't pleased with this one either. *Why am I writing about elite dragons? This is going to be harder than I thought.*

I was having a hard time writing about something that could be universally helpful to all. Each individual's situation was unique and different. Not everyone had the same motivation. Not everyone had family support. I decided that looking for other avenues to help others might be a good idea. Through *Crossover*, I was able to hook up with a well-known mental health advocate that recommended becoming certified as a mental health first aid instructor. I signed up immediately, completed the week-long training, and could now teach others how to become certified in Mental Health First Aid.

LOVE

While my mom was there every day in the recovery at home, Sierra was my main support on the outside. She had a way of making things feel comfortable. She was funny and loyal, not to mention the most beautiful woman I had ever seen. I couldn't help but wonder why she was so into me and stayed by my side while I was at my worst. Her love for me was unconditional.

As months passed with me feeling better and better, Sierra and I decided to make our relationship exclusive while still keeping it light. We genuinely enjoyed each other's company and saw no reason to date other people. I developed the same feelings of love for her that she had for me during this time.

A new construction project began right outside my apartment, which made it very hard for me to get good sleep, something that was so important to my long-term health.

"Why don't you just move in?" she asked.

"Sure," I said.

And that was that. I broke my lease and moved into Sierra's over the next few weeks. I was very happy at her place, it felt like home, and both of our parents were in close proximity.

Sierra told me awhile back that if I ever got her a necklace, she would wear it every day. This statement stuck in my mind, and I knew the perfect gift for Valentine's Day. I picked out a sparkly necklace with the letter *S* on it, and I knew she would love it.

The necklace was a great symbol of our relationship. It represented the bond that we had formed over the eight years that we had known each other through good times and bad. We agreed to stay in that night and enjoy each other's company instead of going out into the cold to a fancy, heavy Valentine's Day meal.

I had one last surprise for Sierra after we ate. I got down on one knee and asked her to marry me.

OWN IT: FOR INDIVIDUALS LIVING WITH BIPOLAR DISORDER

Let's beat this thing.

You are special. You are special because you have insight into something that is mysterious to most people, including medical professionals. You have valuable information that, when processed and organized, can set you apart from others. You see things differently and can push the limits of the human mind. Businesses are scouring the earth to find these types of minds and people with your special type of energy. You have something to celebrate, not be ashamed of. The goal of your personal management plan is to support the way your mind works and create balance, especially with stress.

But you can also be your own worst enemy. You must stop focusing on the things that you *can't* control and direct your attention to the many things that you *can* control. You'll find that the majority of your choices are in your own control when viewing them with a clear perspective. Gaining this perspective takes work and daily maintenance. If you are not prepared to take your chronic brain disorder head-on, then you will not succeed. Of all people with bipolar disorder, 15 percent commit suicide. Get yourself in a headspace that keeps you on the 85 percent side of this statistic. If you are willing to do whatever it takes to live a goal-directed rewarding life, then you can succeed.

You want to feel better. You may be stubborn, pissed off, depressed, and not have any motivation to feel better, but deep down, you really want to experience positive feelings. There is no reason not to want to feel better.

Maybe you aren't ready. It's okay. There is no helping someone who hasn't come to the realization that they are ready to get better on their own. Pushing for steady progress cannot be forced and can, in fact, push people away if applied in the wrong way. Let me remind you that it's okay if you need to take a break for six or more months. It's okay if the thought of trying is painful, exhausting, and makes you feel down. It's okay if the stress is piling on and personal issues outside your bipolar disorder are adding to it.

I believe that if you really dig deep, all the way to your core, you will find a spark that can be nurtured and improved. There is no one else on earth that has seen your exact struggle, which is why you are the only one who has the special recipe to get yourself better. You can do it. You can. When you find that light, I want to help turn it into a flame and then lightning in a bottle for you to unleash at your own pace. I want you to find the new normal, be powerful, and take back what's yours.

You have a 100 percent chance of having another episode if you do not take your meds. One more time: You have a 100 percent chance of having another episode if you do not take your meds. It bothers me that a large chunk of the bipolar population does not take their meds. Taking your meds is one of the easiest things that you can do to manage your illness from a practical perspective. Take them when you are supposed to.

I do not mean to be harsh or insensitive. There is no doubt that taking meds makes you feel crippled, tired, hungry, lethargic, stiff, and more. You must hang in there and take your meds regardless of how off you feel. Getting your meds in order is a very hard part of the process because you are dealing with side effects every time something is adjusted. But know that when you partner with your doctor to work on finding the sweet spot between desirable effects and side effects, you will feel better. One of the worst possible controllable things you can do as a person with bipolar disorder is not follow your doctor's orders while taking meds.

Mastering your meds is mandatory for you now. If you haven't ever needed to take recurring meds, then the pharmacy process can be confusing. Running out of meds is a huge deal because it can lead to you missing multiple doses (which you know by now is one of the worst things that can happen to you). Put simply, have the correct meds and take them at the right time.

Side effects can be brutal. Lithium will make your hands shake and make you have to pee often, even throughout the night. It affects your thyroid, which is managed by Synthroid, a drug without serious side effects but with rules about when to take it before food. Lamictal puts you at risk for a nasty skin condition if not taken properly. You will become dehydrated while taking these drugs, which can cause headaches and dizziness. You must drink water all day to combat this. If you forget to hydrate, you will feel it. Stay the course and know that side effects will not be worse than the result of not taking the medicine—another episode.

You will be asked to get blood work from time to time to ensure that you are tolerating your meds and your levels are within the correct range. Pretend the names of your meds are Red, Blue, and Green. Let's say the levels of each should be between 1 and 2. Your blood work reports will tell the doctor what range you are for Red, Blue, and Green. If Red is 1.5 and Blue is 0.5, then they may need to be adjusted. If Green is 1.0, then it is probably okay as is. This is one factor that your doctor is assessing when prescribing your dosage, and you have the right to ask questions. Ask questions and engage in your treatment plan. The more you understand, the better off you will be outside the doctor's office.

Just like with meds, your doctor will hand you a slip to get your blood work done. You will take this to a public testing facility (like Quest Diagnostics, Lab Corps, or your local hospital), and they will take your blood and get that information back to your doctor. All you have to do is show up with the slip.

You will make mistakes. You will forget to take your dose, take the wrong pill at the wrong time, or run out of medicine altogether.

While it is not ideal, you can easily bounce back without any major issues if it only happens once in a while. There may be a part of you that wants to stop meds altogether when you make one mistake. Don't. Know that managing bipolar disorder is a marathon, and one missed dosage is just a trip-up. Stay strong and go back to being disciplined, reflect on how the mistake was made, and fix it.

There is nothing fun about being told that you will have to take medicine for the rest of your life. But things like taxes and the dentist aren't fun either. Add this to your list of annoying things that you have to do and keep at it. You can do it. You can choose to follow the doctors' orders.

Doctors and therapists are there to help you. They are not money hungry. They are not out to get you. Trust them. You are feeling off because you are working to find the correct balance of chemicals in your body, not because your doctor wants to put you through a painful experience. When you feel that your therapist isn't helping anymore, then you need to dig deeper into yourself. Need to come to your meetings with more insight. Need to open up. You are paying to have a sounding board, so use it. You are responsible for this, not them.

Be honest in these meetings. The system is imperfect in that the professionals must gather information from the patients themselves, the ones who are not thinking clearly. It is our job as the patient to work with professionals, not pout and talk shit behind their backs. We have the disease; they are here to help us. This is the best way that they know how, and we should be grateful that they went through a decade of school for us. They have an interest in learning about our brains. No one else on the planet has this skill set.

You must use this time in meetings to talk about meds, lifestyle, yada yada, but also to learn about yourself and improve as a person. Becoming aware of your issues is critical to your recovery. Surely something has happened in your life since your last visit that made you feel a certain type of way, good or bad. You must ride the good waves and express the bad ones. The thirty- to sixty-minute session is a time to push yourself. Heck, you may not have tried anything else all week long. Here lies another opportunity to make progress while sitting on your ass.

If you have nothing to say, then sit in silence. The act of scheduling and showing up to therapy is a positive thing in itself. Feel the uncomfortable feelings. Observe as your mind brings your issues to light. Swear, cry, get angry, get happy, do nothing, but show up.

Don't lie. You are a logical person. If you tell your doctor that you are feeling a certain way and you are not, then they may prescribe you the wrong medication or dosage. If you are prescribed the wrong medication or dosage, then you've just sabotaged yourself into feeling like shit or having another episode. You are smart. You know what you are doing. Stop indirectly hurting yourself in this way.

You are in a tough situation because you are meeting new people that are going to manipulate the balance of chemicals in your body and know your deepest, darkest secrets. You can either accept this fact and participate or you can blow it off and continue to think that you know what's best for yourself. You will learn about what's best for yourself by working with the doctors and therapists, but without their help, you will be lost, and the disorder will run your life.

Your phone will become more valuable than ever while managing your bipolar disorder. It essentially guarantees that you will be notified when it is time to do whatever it is that you are supposed to do. It will allow you to move events around and view the current day, week, or an entire month.

It is very easy to think big picture and get depressed about being diagnosed with bipolar disorder. Instead of focusing on things that you cannot control, put events on your calendar and do them. On hard days, put one long event that says, "Not leaving the house." But you better still have events like "take meds" on that day. And you better take them. If you mark something on your calendar, then do it. If you forget to schedule something, then fix your own mistakes. This strategy is in your control. You don't need anyone to be the master of your own schedule. This is a great starting point for gaining your independence back.

A major part of being depressed is being too anxious to leave the house yet too restless to stay in the house. It causes a harsh physical feeling paired with emotional guilt that it's your fault. It sucks. You must do the best you can, but please realize that even while depressed, you are spending your time doing something. My hope is that over time, this practice will have you replacing these long periods of depression with the smallest couple minutes of positive activity.

When they first told me to do breathing exercises inside the hospital, I thought, *Fuck off. I already am breathing, and maybe it would be better if I wasn't.* It was too cliché. I don't want to be cliché with you. I want to be real. But guess what? They were right. You should do breathing exercises, meditate, and a bunch of other stuff that will absolutely make you feel better, which is the ultimate goal. If you can manage to build positive activities to your day, then you will feel better. They take mere minutes and do not require you to talk to anyone or even leave the house. Do you feel anxiety building up about doing the activities that I've shared? That's normal. That is normal for anyone who is learning something new, whether they have bipolar disorder or not. I challenge you to get better, not quit, and do these. Don't try them, do them. Schedule them and do them. You can do this. Take some control back and give them a shot.

Your toolbox is empty right now, and you are trying to drive a nail through a shingle on your roof. Square breathing is the hammer that you need. Do this every morning. It takes sixty-four seconds. But even with a hammer, you will not finish the roof without seeing the big picture. You can't just blindly nail shingles and expect to get it done correctly. Meditating will help you know exactly what goes where and why. It's the architectural map of the roof. It's the awareness of what you are doing and why you are doing. Can you do these two things every morning to make yourself feel a bit better? Can you schedule it? Try.

Drugs and alcohol fuck everything up. It's as simple as that. When I have flashbacks of being carted off to the padded room wearing a straitjacket in the psych ward, I am motivated to not fuck everything up and put myself back in that position. What is your lowest point? Hold this moment in your mind for a minute.

Understand that you are moving toward this moment every time that you use drugs or alcohol. Not taking your meds is the worst, but mixing your meds with drugs and alcohol is a close second. If you are using drugs or alcohol, then you have no right to blame the world for your bipolar disorder. You cannot have it both ways. Either decide to live a rewarding life and make decisions that fall in line with that or continue to use drugs and alcohol and know that you are the reason that you are stuck, not the disorder. I struggle to find the right amount of forcefulness behind communicating how I feel about people who are bipolar and still use drugs and alcohol. My story is most likely much different from yours, and I'm sure you have your reasons.

You are probably thinking, *So what? Have a drink or two at the bar. It's not a big deal.* But it is. If I allow myself the wiggle room to have a drink or two, then I am setting the bar at a place where I can drink and add to my tolerance. Two drinks can mean a lot of different things, and when buzzed off, two drinks, three drinks, doesn't seem like a big deal and so on. Remember that your body has changed and is on medicine forever. Adding drugs and alcohol can only make things worse.

You must decide what sacrifices you are willing to make to avoid your lowest point and live a content and rewarding life. Enough random, unlucky things will happen to you on your journey. Do not sabotage yourself by using drugs and alcohol. You do not deserve sympathy or attention if your meds aren't working after a night of drinking or using drugs. Take the tough love and stop. It will not be easy, but you must do it to avoid being part of the 15 percent.

You can be doing everything right and still trigger an episode by being unaware of your sleep. It's important that you are conscious of how many hours you are getting every twenty-four-hour cycle. Things like caffeine and energy drinks are seemingly harmless when compared to drugs and alcohol, but they can kill your ability to sleep, which is dangerous for you.

Taking meds and cutting out drugs and alcohol are the obvious wins when managing bipolar disorder. But many overlook the amount of sleep that they are getting. It's a hidden trigger that is worth being aware of and reporting to your doctor. Episodes can come on hyper fast, but for me, they only occurred when I had little or no sleep for a few days in a row. You must make every effort to get sleep and be aware if you are unable to sleep from here on out.

Making connections is a key factor in taming isolation. Practically speaking, when you create bonds there are more people checking in and aware if your behavior has turned. These bonds alone will not prevent an episode, but it's important to have an awareness of who is in your life and how deep your connections go.

Stress will always be there. That pulling in your chest. That worry that things will not be okay. Stress is major and is not something to be overlooked. Isolation, lack of sleep, and stress were the trio that spun me into my third manic episode.

Be sure to sort out what is causing the stress. You do not have to solve the internal issues on your own, but do you know what the issue is? When I feel stressed, I lean heavily on my doctor and therapist. I release ownership of it and simply communicate what I'm feeling to them. It's their job to help you relieve some of this stress. At the very least, you'll begin to develop an understanding of where the stress comes from. Everyone can benefit from this exercise, bipolar or not. Getting to the core of this uncomfortable feeling is an important step in conquering the unique set of issues that you are faced with.

Working out is the worst. It sucks. It hurts. It's hard. But no one can argue that no matter how shitty one feels going into a workout, they always feel better afterward. It's obviously healthy, good for you, blah, blah, blah, but everyone is at a different level and the motivational bullshit gets old. But the benefits of exercise are huge. Exercise clears your mind, focuses your attention, helps set your sleep schedule, and burns calories. It can also get you out of the house in a recurring way.

You must make progress. If you've been in bed for six months, then getting out of bed is progress. If you've been taking five-minute walks every day, then six minutes is progress. If you've been running marathons and doing iron man competitions, then chill out because you are making the rest of us feel bad! The point here, again, is to have an awareness of where you are today.

You should reward yourself with a small treat like a scoop of ice cream, candy bar, small bag of chips, or something else in this wheelhouse if you make progress. The best time to eat unhealthy food that you love is right after a workout. You have deeper struggles happening right now to manage your bipolar disorder, like taking your medication, staying away from drugs and alcohol, and getting enough sleep. But the food and exercise part of your healthy balance is important too.

Hold yourself accountable. Know that if you make progress in your workouts that you get a reward at the end. You have full control over this. No workout, no reward. There is a scenario that plays out where you skip your workout but eat unhealthy food anyway. This will most certainly lead to guilt, which is a crippling feeling.

Be aware of the cycles that your body goes through. Know that when you commit to making progress in your workouts that you will get that reward and do not have to feel guilty. Stack this healthy cycle on top of the medication regimen that you are getting comfortable with and avoiding drugs and alcohol and you will have something to feel proud of.

And look out if you feel pride. Pride can be lightning in a bottle. Someone with your special brain can be dangerously productive and move very fast with this small kick. Look out, world.

You have so many things working against you when it comes to food because it's one of the few things that still feels normal and gives you satisfaction. A slice of pizza is delicious before, during, and after a manic episode. Your medication is making you hungrier than ever. There's also a lot of guilt associated with food, mainly after the meal is over. Remember that if you are taking your medication and staying away from drugs and alcohol, then you are already kicking ass; feel good about that. You can figure your diet out as well, and extra weight can shed quickly. This issue is emotional, logical, and must be prioritized. You have no reason to feel guilty.

You don't need to change anything today, but you must add to your self-awareness about what is actually happening. This is not about your being weak, fake, or less than. This is about a new chemical being introduced into your body. A chemical that you are brave enough to take and trust others about taking. That deep, dark, feeling is hard to overcome. Eat slowly and enjoy your food. Take every ounce of happiness that it will give you. Do not blame yourself. You must break the emotional guilt in order to make changes to your diet. Start by doing that.

There is a balanced light at the end of the tunnel here that allows you to enjoy your food, not overeat, and feel good about your diet all while being on meds and avoiding drugs and alcohol. Remember that we are running a marathon together. Find that part of you deep inside that feels guilty about what you eat and confront it. You will come back to the issue of food often, but you may be battling bigger issues right now. That's okay. Know that it's nothing to feel bad about.

There was a time in your past when you had fun doing things. Things like dancing, photography, biking, bowling, golfing, hiking, skating, skiing, swimming, fishing, kayaking, camping, running, gaming, playing sports, hanging out with friends, and more. Now they aren't fun. Now the thought of even trying them is uncomfortable. Like with your workouts and diet, finding something to devote your time to requires an awareness that progress must be made.

In order to make this progress, you must see the hidden barrier that you are up against. But you can push back. You can make progress. You can ask yourself, *What is the worst thing that happens?* The answer might be a scary one. "I'll feel bad," "I'll fail," "I'll be embarrassed," etc. But remember, you are already taming the beast that is bipolar disorder, and you are now thinking about taking a huge step of getting back out there. Again, that is a major success that should be celebrated. Like before, if it's too much, then take some time to regroup and stay on your health routines. Do not allow forecasting and fear to stop you from taking your meds or start using drugs and alcohol. You are strong and will find something that you like doing when the time is right.

You must understand that whether you are making money or not, getting out and doing some sort of work is helping you tremendously. It's allowing yourself to build confidence until the next opportunity arises. After you get comfortable in the volunteering arena, finding a paying job will be much easier.

Don't forget that all five of your senses are just scrambled. You are seeing things that aren't there, hearing voices, smelling false smells, feeling false feels, and tasting false tastes. These past experiences will greatly affect your ability to get back out there and socialize. And for good reason. There is nothing more embarrassing than acting funny in public. If your episode was public, then you are on the far end of a spectrum with not a care in the world of what people thinks of you. But now you are back to reality and the world looks much more intimidating. You are vulnerable and unsure about your own behavior. Be aware of your private versus public thoughts and know that you never have to share something that you don't want to. You'll learn how to navigate these tricky social waters overtime.

Having the confidence to not only get back out there and socialize, but also without using alcohol as a crutch, is the pinnacle of self-confidence. It shows that you are fully comfortable in your own skin. Most people in general do not have this confidence.

Having a social life when you have bipolar disorder is not something to force. At the end of the day, you just might not feel good when you are out. It's not something that people can make you do. Do not allow your struggles with social stuff affect other parts of your regimen. Do not spiral and stop taking your meds because you feel uncomfortable around friends. You may navigate this arena, maybe for an extended period of time, before finding your place. I can assure you, however, that when you have your routine in place, things begin to seem easier, you can feel proud about all the things you are handling, and that social confidence may present itself without you even realizing it.

Let me remind you that you have a chronic health condition. It's never going away. You'll be reminded of it every day, and many of the tasks throughout your day will be dedicated to managing it. It's a major accomplishment to handle all this, and you should feel good about that. If the only achievement you have for the rest of your life is appropriately managing your bipolar disorder, then you've done a kick-ass job. No one can take that away from you. The hard part is that this is your new baseline. You have to handle all this stuff just to get even.

Gaining your independence is huge. It means that you have developed enough of a routine and skills to manage your bipolar disorder. If some other part of your life is getting you down, you must remember that you are already winning if you have this stuff in order and are avoiding episodes by keeping yourself in check on the bipolar side of things.

You must bring your game to the next level when you become independent. You may get a phone call or two from loved ones that are checking in and seeing how you are doing. You may have in-home support from your spouse and family. But we both know that in order for you to truly be up and running, the heavy lifting is done by you on a daily basis. Breathing exercises, medicine, mediation, healthy diet, no drugs or alcohol, doctors and therapists, sleep, and much more; this is all up to you.

But when you find that sweet spot, that spot where your body sees no other way than the way things, are right now, you are truly independent. You have let go of the pain from the past, and you are able to enjoy moments in the present, like anyone else would.

The long run is longer than you think. This means that things can always improve. You can always add to your repertoire and share what's working with others. But be selfish first, get your routine in order, and gain your independence. Be proud of what you've accomplished. There will be ups and downs, but you can always fall back into your routine.

It's one thing to learn a few tips and have a general understanding about how to live a rewarding life with bipolar disorder. It's another to hold yourself accountable and have the discipline to be successful. You must look at the management of your bipolar disorder as a new job that you are qualified for. Here is the job description:

Newly Diagnosed Bipolar Individual
Director of Oneself
Reports to Medical Professionals
Job Overview

The purpose of this role is to successfully manage one's own bipolar disorder with the goal of living a healthy, rewarding life. Success in the role is the individual performing learned skills and progressive behaviors that allow for prevention of future episodes. The individual's achievements will move the needle and provide inspiration to others affected by the illness.

Responsibilities and Duties

- Take medicine
- Eliminate drugs and alcohol
- Develop morning routine
- Work out
- Get Sleep
- Learn and grow overtime

Qualifications

- Must have a bipolar diagnosis
- No education required
- No experience necessary
- No advanced skills necessary
- Must be open minded
- Must try

We've taken some time to feel bad for ourselves because we've been diagnosed with bipolar disorder. We've taken as much time as we needed because we are in the 2 percent of the population that have an exponentially greater risk of suicide, no guarantees on our long-term health, and have had a hard time helping others understand what we go through on a daily basis. We have lost confidence, struggled to regain our independence, and have been suffocated by what-ifs. We have thoroughly experienced a challenging period of acceptance and are ready to take a look at what our world is like now.

We are special. We are special because we have insight into something that is mysterious to most people, including medical professionals. We have valuable information that, when organized, can set us apart. We see things differently and can push the limits of the human mind. Businesses are scouring the earth to find this special type of energy and people with these types of minds. We have one, and it's something to celebrate, not be ashamed of. The goal is to support the way our mind works and create balance.

But we can be our own worst enemy. We must understand that there are many things that we can control. We must stop focusing on the things that we can't control. We've known that the majority of our choices are in our own control when viewing them with a clear perspective. Gaining this perspective takes work and daily maintenance. We are prepared to take our chronic brain disorder head-on, and we will succeed. Of all people with bipolar disorder, 15 percent commit suicide. We will get ourselves in a headspace that keeps you on the 85 percent side of this statistic. We are willing to do whatever it takes to live a rewarding life and we will.

My Fight Back

Weekly Schedule	Sunday	Monday	Tuesday	Wednesday	Thursday	Friday	Saturday

Weekly Schedule	Sunday	Monday	Tuesday	Wednesday	Thursday	Friday	Saturday
9:00 a.m.	Meds	Meds	Meds	Meds	Meds	Meds	Meds
2:00 p.m.	Meds	Meds	Meds	Meds	Meds	Meds	Meds
9:00 p.m.	Meds	Meds	Meds	Meds	Meds	Meds	Meds

Weekly Schedule	Sunday	Monday	Tuesday	Wednesday	Thursday	Friday	Saturday
9:00 a.m.	Meds	Meds	Meds	Meds	Meds	Meds	Meds
10:00 a.m.			Psychiatrist		Therapist		
2:00 p.m.	Meds	Meds	Meds	Meds	Meds	Meds	Meds
9:00 p.m.	Meds	Meds	Meds	Meds	Meds	Meds	Meds

Weekly Schedule	Sunday	Monday	Tuesday	Wednesday	Thursday	Friday	Saturday
	Lucky to be alive	Lucky to be alive	Lucky to be alive	Lucky to be alive	Lucky to be alive	Lucky to be alive	Lucky to be alive
9:00 a.m.	Wake up, Make Bed, Brush Teeth, Shower, Eat Breakfast, Take Meds	Wake up, Make Bed, Brush Teeth, Shower, Eat Breakfast, Take Meds	Wake up, Make Bed, Brush Teeth, Shower, Eat Breakfast, Take Meds	Wake up, Make Bed, Brush Teeth, Shower, Eat Breakfast, Take Meds	Wake up, Make Bed, Brush Teeth, Shower, Eat Breakfast, Take Meds	Wake up, Make Bed, Brush Teeth, Shower, Eat Breakfast, Take Meds	Wake up, Make Bed, Brush Teeth, Shower, Eat Breakfast, Take Meds
10:00 a.m.			Psychiatrist		Therapist		
2:00 p.m.	Meds	Meds	Meds	Meds	Meds	Meds	Meds
9:00 p.m.	Meds	Meds	Meds	Meds	Meds	Meds	Meds

CROSSING BACK OVER THE PRACTICE OF OWNING AND ACCEPTING BIPOLAR DISORDER

Weekly Schedule	Sunday	Monday	Tuesday	Wednesday	Thursday	Friday	Saturday
	Lucky to be alive	Lucky to be alive	Lucky to be alive	Lucky to be alive	Lucky to be alive	Lucky to be alive	Lucky to be alive
9:00 a.m.	Wake up, Make Bed, Brush Teeth, Shower, Do Square Breathing, Eat Breakfast, Take Meds	Wake up, Make Bed, Brush Teeth, Shower, Do Square Breathing, Eat Breakfast, Take Meds	Wake up, Make Bed, Brush Teeth, Shower, Do Square Breathing, Eat Breakfast, Take Meds	Wake up, Make Bed, Brush Teeth, Shower, Do Square Breathing, Eat Breakfast, Take Meds	Wake up, Make Bed, Brush Teeth, Shower, Do Square Breathing, Eat Breakfast, Take Meds	Wake up, Make Bed, Brush Teeth, Shower, Do Square Breathing, Eat Breakfast, Take Meds	Wake up, Make Bed, Brush Teeth, Shower, Do Square Breathing, Eat Breakfast, Take Meds
10:00 a.m.			Psychiatrist		Therapist		
2:00 p.m.	Square Breathing, Meds	Square Breathing, Meds	Square Breathing, Meds	Square Breathing, Meds	Square Breathing, Meds	Square Breathing, Meds	Square Breathing, Meds
9:00 p.m.	Square Breathing, Meds	Square Breathing, Meds	Square Breathing, Meds	Square Breathing, Meds	Square Breathing, Meds	Square Breathing, Meds	Square Breathing, Meds

Weekly Schedule	Sunday	Monday	Tuesday	Wednesday	Thursday	Friday	Saturday
9:00 a.m.	Wake up, Make Bed, Brush Teeth, Shower, Do Square Breathing, Meditate, Eat Breakfast, Take Meds	Wake up, Make Bed, Brush Teeth, Shower, Do Square Breathing, Meditate, Eat Breakfast, Take Meds	Wake up, Make Bed, Brush Teeth, Shower, Do Square Breathing, Meditate, Eat Breakfast, Take Meds	Wake up, Make Bed, Brush Teeth, Shower, Do Square Breathing, Meditate, Eat Breakfast, Take Meds	Wake up, Make Bed, Brush Teeth, Shower, Do Square Breathing, Meditate, Eat Breakfast, Take Meds	Wake up, Make Bed, Brush Teeth, Shower, Do Square Breathing, Meditate, Eat Breakfast, Take Meds	Wake up, Make Bed, Brush Teeth, Shower, Do Square Breathing, Meditate, Eat Breakfast, Take Meds
10:00 a.m.			Psychiatrist		Therapist		
2:00 p.m.	Square Breathing, Meds	Square Breathing, Meds	Square Breathing, Meds	Square Breathing, Meds	Square Breathing, Meds	Square Breathing, Meds	Square Breathing, Meds
9:00 p.m.	Square Breathing, Meds	Square Breathing, Meds	Square Breathing, Meds	Square Breathing, Meds	Square Breathing, Meds	Square Breathing, Meds	Square Breathing, Meds

Weekly Schedule	Sunday	Monday	Tuesday	Wednesday	Thursday	Friday	Saturday
	Lucky to be alive	Lucky to be alive	Lucky to be alive	Lucky to be alive	Lucky to be alive	Lucky to be alive	Lucky to be alive
9:00 a.m.	Wake up, Take Synthroid, Make Bed, Brush Teeth, Shower, Do Square Breathing, Meditate, Eat Breakfast, Take Meds	Wake up, Take Synthroid, Make Bed, Brush Teeth, Shower, Do Square Breathing, Meditate, Eat Breakfast, Take Meds	Wake up, Take Synthroid, Make Bed, Brush Teeth, Shower, Do Square Breathing, Meditate, Eat Breakfast, Take Meds	Wake up, Take Synthroid, Make Bed, Brush Teeth, Shower, Do Square Breathing, Meditate, Eat Breakfast, Take Meds	Wake up, Take Synthroid, Make Bed, Brush Teeth, Shower, Do Square Breathing, Meditate, Eat Breakfast, Take Meds	Wake up, Take Synthroid, Make Bed, Brush Teeth, Shower, Do Square Breathing, Meditate, Eat Breakfast, Take Meds	Wake up, Take Synthroid, Make Bed, Brush Teeth, Shower, Do Square Breathing, Meditate, Eat Breakfast, Take Meds
10:00 a.m.			Psychiatrist		Therapist		
2:00 p.m.	Square Breathing, Meds	Square Breathing, Meds	Square Breathing, Meds	Square Breathing, Meds	Square Breathing, Meds	Square Breathing, Meds	Square Breathing, Meds
9:00 p.m.	Square Breathing, Meds	Square Breathing, Meds	Square Breathing, Meds	Square Breathing, Meds	Square Breathing, Meds	Square Breathing, Meds	Square Breathing, Meds

Weekly Schedule	Sunday	Monday	Tuesday	Wednesday	Thursday	Friday	Saturday
	Lucky to be alive	Lucky to be alive	Lucky to be alive	Lucky to be alive	Lucky to be alive	Lucky to be alive	Lucky to be alive
9:00 a.m.	Wake up, Take Synthroid, Make Bed, Brush Teeth, Shower, Do Square Breathing, Meditate, Eat Breakfast, Take Meds	Wake up, Take Synthroid, Make Bed, Brush Teeth, Shower, Do Square Breathing, Meditate, Eat Breakfast, Take Meds	Wake up, Take Synthroid, Make Bed, Brush Teeth, Shower, Do Square Breathing, Meditate, Eat Breakfast, Take Meds	Wake up, Take Synthroid, Make Bed, Brush Teeth, Shower, Do Square Breathing, Meditate, Eat Breakfast, Take Meds	Wake up, Take Synthroid, Make Bed, Brush Teeth, Shower, Do Square Breathing, Meditate, Eat Breakfast, Take Meds	Wake up, Take Synthroid, Make Bed, Brush Teeth, Shower, Do Square Breathing, Meditate, Eat Breakfast, Take Meds	Wake up, Take Synthroid, Make Bed, Brush Teeth, Shower, Do Square Breathing, Meditate, Eat Breakfast, Take Meds
10:00 a.m.			Psychiatrist		Therapist		
2:00 p.m.	Square Breathing, Meds	Square Breathing, Meds	Square Breathing, Meds	Square Breathing, Meds	Square Breathing, Meds	Square Breathing, Meds	Square Breathing, Meds
3:00 p.m.	Workout	Workout	Workout	Workout	Workout	Workout	Workout
9:00 p.m.	Square Breathing, Meds	Square Breathing, Meds	Square Breathing, Meds	Square Breathing, Meds	Square Breathing, Meds	Square Breathing, Meds	Square Breathing, Meds

Weekly Schedule	Sunday	Monday	Tuesday	Wednesday	Thursday	Friday	Saturday
	Lucky to be alive	Lucky to be alive	Lucky to be alive	Lucky to be alive	Lucky to be alive	Lucky to be alive	Lucky to be alive
9:00 a.m.	Wake up, Take Synthroid, Make Bed, Brush Teeth, Shower, Do Square Breathing, Meditate, Eat Breakfast, Take Meds	Wake up, Take Synthroid, Make Bed, Brush Teeth, Shower, Do Square Breathing, Meditate, Eat Breakfast, Take Meds	Wake up, Take Synthroid, Make Bed, Brush Teeth, Shower, Do Square Breathing, Meditate, Eat Breakfast, Take Meds	Wake up, Take Synthroid, Make Bed, Brush Teeth, Shower, Do Square Breathing, Meditate, Eat Breakfast, Take Meds	Wake up, Take Synthroid, Make Bed, Brush Teeth, Shower, Do Square Breathing, Meditate, Eat Breakfast, Take Meds	Wake up, Take Synthroid, Make Bed, Brush Teeth, Shower, Do Square Breathing, Meditate, Eat Breakfast, Take Meds	Wake up, Take Synthroid, Make Bed, Brush Teeth, Shower, Do Square Breathing, Meditate, Eat Breakfast, Take Meds
10:00 a.m.	The Poker Project	The Poker Project	Psychiatrist then The Poker Project	The Poker Project	Therapist then The Poker Project	The Poker Project	The Poker Project
2:00 p.m.	Square Breathing, Meds	Square Breathing, Meds	Square Breathing, Meds	Square Breathing, Meds	Square Breathing, Meds	Square Breathing, Meds	Square Breathing, Meds
3:00 p.m.	Workout	Workout	Workout	Workout	Workout	Workout	Workout
9:00 p.m.	Square Breathing, Meds	Square Breathing, Meds	Square Breathing, Meds	Square Breathing, Meds	Square Breathing, Meds	Square Breathing, Meds	Square Breathing, Meds

Weekly Schedule	Sunday	Monday	Tuesday	Wednesday	Thursday	Friday	Saturday
	Lucky to be alive	Lucky to be alive	Lucky to be alive	Lucky to be alive	Lucky to be alive	Lucky to be alive	Lucky to be alive
9:00 a.m.	Wake up, Take Synthroid, Make Bed, Brush Teeth, Shower, Do Square Breathing, Meditate, Eat Breakfast, Take Meds	Wake up, Take Synthroid, Make Bed, Brush Teeth, Shower, Do Square Breathing, Meditate, Eat Breakfast, Take Meds	Wake up, Take Synthroid, Make Bed, Brush Teeth, Shower, Do Square Breathing, Meditate, Eat Breakfast, Take Meds	Wake up, Take Synthroid, Make Bed, Brush Teeth, Shower, Do Square Breathing, Meditate, Eat Breakfast, Take Meds	Wake up, Take Synthroid, Make Bed, Brush Teeth, Shower, Do Square Breathing, Meditate, Eat Breakfast, Take Meds	Wake up, Take Synthroid, Make Bed, Brush Teeth, Shower, Do Square Breathing, Meditate, Eat Breakfast, Take Meds	Wake up, Take Synthroid, Make Bed, Brush Teeth, Shower, Do Square Breathing, Meditate, Eat Breakfast, Take Meds
10:00 a.m.			Psychiatrist		Therapist then The Poker Project		
11:00 a.m.				Chess	The Poker Project		
2:00 p.m.	Square Breathing, Meds	Square Breathing, Meds	Square Breathing, Meds	Square Breathing, Meds	Square Breathing, Meds	Square Breathing, Meds	Square Breathing, Meds
3:00 p.m.	Workout	Workout	Workout	Workout	Workout	Workout	Workout
9:00 p.m.	Square Breathing, Meds	Square Breathing, Meds	Square Breathing, Meds	Square Breathing, Meds	Square Breathing, Meds	Square Breathing, Meds	Square Breathing, Meds

Weekly Schedule	Sunday	Monday	Tuesday	Wednesday	Thursday	Friday	Saturday
	Lucky to be alive	Lucky to be alive	Lucky to be alive	Lucky to be alive	Lucky to be alive	Lucky to be alive	Lucky to be alive
9:00 a.m.	Wake up, Take Synthroid, Make Bed, Brush Teeth, Shower, Do Square Breathing, Meditate, Eat Breakfast, Take Meds	Wake up, Take Synthroid, Make Bed, Brush Teeth, Shower, Do Square Breathing, Meditate, Eat Breakfast, Take Meds	Wake up, Take Synthroid, Make Bed, Brush Teeth, Shower, Do Square Breathing, Meditate, Eat Breakfast, Take Meds	Wake up, Take Synthroid, Make Bed, Brush Teeth, Shower, Do Square Breathing, Meditate, Eat Breakfast, Take Meds	Wake up, Take Synthroid, Make Bed, Brush Teeth, Shower, Do Square Breathing, Meditate, Eat Breakfast, Take Meds	Wake up, Take Synthroid, Make Bed, Brush Teeth, Shower, Do Square Breathing, Meditate, Eat Breakfast, Take Meds	Wake up, Take Synthroid, Make Bed, Brush Teeth, Shower, Do Square Breathing, Meditate, Eat Breakfast, Take Meds
10:00 a.m.		Psychiatrist			Therapist then The Poker Project		
11:00 a.m.				Chess	The Poker Project		
2:00 p.m.	Square Breathing, Meds	Square Breathing, Meds	Square Breathing, Meds	Square Breathing, Meds	Square Breathing, Meds	Square Breathing, Meds	Square Breathing, Meds
3:00 p.m.	Workout	Workout	Workout	Workout	Workout	Workout	Workout
9:00 p.m.	Square Breathing, Meds	Square Breathing, Meds	Square Breathing, Meds	Square Breathing, Meds	Square Breathing, Meds	Square Breathing, Meds	Square Breathing, Meds

Weekly Schedule	Sunday	Monday	Tuesday	Wednesday	Thursday	Friday	Saturday
	Lucky to be alive	Lucky to be alive	Lucky to be alive	Lucky to be alive	Lucky to be alive	Lucky to be alive	Lucky to be alive
9:00 a.m.	Wake up, Take Synthroid, Make Bed, Brush Teeth, Shower, Do Square Breathing, Meditate, Eat Breakfast, Take Meds	Wake up, Take Synthroid, Make Bed, Brush Teeth, Shower, Do Square Breathing, Meditate, Eat Breakfast, Take Meds	Wake up, Take Synthroid, Make Bed, Brush Teeth, Shower, Do Square Breathing, Meditate, Eat Breakfast, Take Meds	Wake up, Take Synthroid, Make Bed, Brush Teeth, Shower, Do Square Breathing, Meditate, Eat Breakfast, Take Meds	Wake up, Take Synthroid, Make Bed, Brush Teeth, Shower, Do Square Breathing, Meditate, Eat Breakfast, Take Meds	Wake up, Take Synthroid, Make Bed, Brush Teeth, Shower, Do Square Breathing, Meditate, Eat Breakfast, Take Meds	Wake up, Take Synthroid, Make Bed, Brush Teeth, Shower, Do Square Breathing, Meditate, Eat Breakfast, Take Meds
10:00 a.m.			Psychiatrist		Therapist	The Poker Project	
11:00 a.m.			Workout	Chess	Workout	The Poker Project	
2:00 p.m.	Square Breathing, Meds	Square Breathing, Meds	Square Breathing, Meds, Volunteer	Square Breathing, Meds	Square Breathing, Meds, Volunteer	Square Breathing, Meds	Square Breathing, Meds
3:00 p.m.	Workout	Workout	Volunteer	Workout	Volunteer	Workout	Workout
9:00 p.m.	Square Breathing, Meds	Square Breathing, Meds	Square Breathing, Meds	Square Breathing, Meds	Square Breathing, Meds	Square Breathing, Meds	Square Breathing, Meds

ABOUT THE AUTHOR

Brett Stevens is a thirty-three-year-old author who has written this follow-up memoir describing his personal experience with bipolar I disorder recovery. This story follows his first book, *Crossover: A Look Inside a Manic Mind*, which starts out as a therapeutic exercise to write a narrative of his life, integrating his childhood memories with the visceral accounts of recurrent major psychiatric illness in adulthood. Along the way, he discovers that he has hypermnesia: the incredible ability to remember personal life events with detailed accuracy. As a result, this first-person account details Brett's battle with depression, anxiety, loss of independence, and what it takes to find a happy life while living with bipolar disorder. Brett is the middle of three sons born to an affluent family who lives comfortably in an upper-middle-class neighborhood. Despite being derailed with three psychotic episodes, he finishes college and has found success in three separate careers: professional poker, health club sales administration, and most recently, real estate. He has written a poker blog and developed an online program to teach others how to play. He also competes at amateur chess. He enjoys teaching and training others, and he is deeply committed to helping other people who struggle with Bipolar I disorder.

CPSIA information can be obtained
at www.ICGtesting.com
Printed in the USA
LVHW090900221120
672356LV00022B/162/J